PIECES OF HATE

HEYWOOD BROUN

PIECES OF HATE
And Other Enthusiasms
By HEYWOOD BROUN

WILDSIDE PRESS

www.wildsidepress.com

TO MY FATHER
HEYWOOD C. BROUN

PREFACE

The trouble with prefaces is that they are partial and so we have decided to offer instead an unbiased review of "Pieces of Hate." The publishers have kindly furnished us advance proofs for this purpose.

We wish we could speak with unreserved enthusiasm about this book. It would be pleasant to make out a list of three essential volumes for humanity and suggest the complete works of William Shakespeare, the Bible and "Pieces of Hate," but Mr. Broun's book does not deserve any such ranking. Speaking as a critic of books, we are not at all sure that we care to recommend it. It seems to us that the author is honest, but the value of that quality has been vastly overstressed in present-day reviewing. We are inclined to say "What of it?" There would be nothing particularly persuasive if a man should approach a poker game and say, "Won't you let Broun in; I can assure he's honest." Why should a recommendation which is taken for granted among common gamblers be considered flattering when applied to a writer?

Anyhow, it does not seem to us that Broun carries honesty to excess. There is every indication that most of the work in "Pieces of Hate" has been done so hurriedly that there has been no opportunity for a recount. If it balances at any given

point luck must be with him as well as virtue. All
the vices of haste are in this book of stories, critical
essays and what not. The author is not content to
stalk down an idea and salt it. Whenever he sees
what he believes to be a notion he leaves his feet and
tries to bring it down with a flying tackle. Occasionally there actually is an exciting and interesting
crash of flying bodies coming into contact. But just
as often Mr. Broun misses his mark and falls on his
face. At other times he gets the object of his dive
only to find that it was not a genuine idea after all,
but only a straw man, a sort of tackling dummy set
up to fool and educate novices.

And Broun does not learn fast. Like most newspaper persons he is an extraordinary mixture of
sophistication and naïveté. At one moment he will
be found belaboring a novelist or a dramatist for
sentimentality and on the next page there will be
distinct traces of treacle in his own creative work.
Seemingly, what he means when he says that he does
not like sentimentality is that he doesn't like the sentimentality of anybody else. He would restrict the
quality to the same narrow field as charity.

The various forms introduced into the book are a
little confusing. Seemingly there has been no plan
as to the sequence of stories, essays, dramatic criticism and the rest. Possibly the author regards this
as versatility, but here is another vastly overrated
quality. We once had a close friend who was a
magician and after we had watched him take an
omelet out of his high hat, and two white rabbits, and
a bowl of goldfish, it always made us a little uneasy

PREFACE

when he said, "Wait a minute until I put on my hat and I'll walk home with you."

The fear constantly lurked in our mind that he might suddenly remember, in the middle of Times Square, that he had forgotten a trick and be compelled to pause and take a boa-constrictor from under the sweat-band. We suggest to Mr. Broun that he make up his mind as to just what he intends to do and then stick to it to the exclusion of all sidelines.

Perhaps he has promised, but we are prepared to wager nothing on him until we are convinced that he has begun to drive for something. He may be a young man but he is not so young that he can afford to traffic any further with flipness under the impression that it is something just as good as humor. And we wish he wouldn't pun. George H. Doran, the publisher, informs us that he had to plead with Broun to make him leave out a chapter on the ugliness of heirlooms and particularly old sofas. Apparently the piece was written for no other purpose than to carry the title "The Chintz of the Fathers."

We also find Mr. Broun's pose as the professional Harvard man a little bit trying, particularly as expressed in his essay "The Bigger the Year." We suppose he may be expected to outgrow this in time but he has been long enough about it."

HEYWOOD BROUN.

Some of these articles have appeared in the *New York World*, the *New York Tribune*, *Vanity Fair*, *Collier's Weekly*, *The Bookman* and *Judge*, and acknowledgment is made to these publications for permission to reprint.

CONTENTS

CONTENTS

PIECES OF HATE

I

THE NOT IMPOSSIBLE SHEIK

Women must be peculiar people, if that. We have just finished "The Sheik," which is described on the jacket as possessing "ALL the intense passion and tender feeling of the most vivid love stories, almost brutal in its revelations."

Naturally, we read it. The author is English and named E. M. Hull. The publishers expand the "E" to Ethel, but we have a theory of our own. At any rate the novelist displays an extraordinary knowledge of feminine psychology. It is profound. It is also a little disturbing because it sounds so silly. After all, whether peculiar or not women are round about us almost everywhere, and we must make the best of them. Accordingly, it terrifies us to learn that if by any chance whatsoever we happen to hit one of them and knock her down she will become devoted to us forever. The man who knows this will think twice before he strikes a woman no matter what the provocation. He will be inclined to count ten before letting a blow go instead of after. Miss Hull's book deserves the widest possible circulation because of its persuasive propaganda for forebearance on the part of men in their dealings with women.

Seemingly, there are no exceptions to the rules about women laid down by Miss Hull. To state her theory concisely, the quickest way to reach a woman's heart is a right hook to the jaw. To take a specific instance, there was Miss Diana Mayo. She seemed an exception to the rule if ever a woman did. "My God, Diana! Beauty like yours drives a man mad!" said Arbuthnot, the young British lieutenant, in the moonlight at Biskra. More than that, "He whispered ardently, his hands closing over the slim ones lying in her lap." Those were her own.

Still, Diana was no miss to take a hint. With a strength that seemed impossible for their slimness she disengaged her hands from his grasp. "Please stop. I am sorry. We have been good friends, and it has never occurred to me that there could be anything beyond that. I never thought that you might love me. I never thought of you in that way at all. I don't understand it. When God made me he omitted to give me a heart. I have never loved any one in my life."

That was before Miss Diana Mayo went into the desert and met the Sheik Ahmed Ben Hassan. The meeting was unconventional. Ahmed sacked the caravan and kidnapped Diana, seizing her off her horse's back at full gallop. "His movement had been so quick she was unprepared and unable to resist. For a moment she was stunned, then her senses came back to her and she struggled wildly, but stifled in the thick folds of the Arab's robes, against which her face was crushed, and held in a grip that seemed to be slowly suffocating her, her struggles were futile. The hard, muscular arm around her hurt her acutely, her ribs seemed to be almost breaking under its weight and strength, it was nearly impossible to breathe with the close contact of his body."

But Diana did not love him yet. She seems to have been less susceptible than most girls. Even when "her whole body was one agonized ache from the brutal hands" she persisted in not caring for Ahmed Ben Hassan. It almost seemed as if she had taken a dislike to the man. Up to this time she had not learned to make allowances for him. It was much later than this that "She looked at the marks of his fingers on the delicate skin with a twist of the lips, then shut her eyes with a little gasp and hid her bruised arm hastily, her mouth quivering. But she did not blame him; she had brought it on herself; she knew his mood and he did not know his own strength."

Diana's realization that she loved the Sheik Ahmed Ben Hassan and had loved him for some time came under sudden and dramatic circumstances. She was running away from him at the time and he was riding after her. Standing up in the stirrups, the Sheik shot the horse from under her and "Diana was flung far forward and landed on some soft sand." But even yet her blindness to the whispering of love persisted. She thought she hated Ahmed, but dawn was about to break in her starved heart. "He caught her wrist and flung her out of the way," yet it was not until he had lifted her up on the saddle in front

19

of him, using his favorite hold—a half nelson and body scissors—that the punishing nature of the familiar grip roused Diana to an understanding of her great good fortune. "Quite suddenly she knew— knew that she loved him, that she had loved him for a long time, even when she thought that she hated him and when she had fled from him. She knew now why his face had haunted her in the little oasis at midday—that it was love calling to her sub-consciously." And all the time poor, foolish Diana had imagined that it was arnica which she wanted.

Even after Ben Hassan had succeeded in impress-ing Diana with his affection, we feared that the story would not end happily. While riding some miles away from their own carefully restricted oasis Diana was captured by another Arab chief named Ibraheim Omair. It seemed to us that he was in his way just as persuasive a wooer as Ben Hassan. We read, "He forced her to her knees, and, with his hand twined brutally in her curls, thrust her head back," and later, "She realized that he was squeezing the life out of her." Worst of all from the point of view of a Ben Hassan partisan (and by this time we too had learned to love him) was the moment in which Omair dashed his hand against Diana's mouth, for the author records that "She caught it in her teeth, biting it to the bone." We feared, then, that Diana's heart was turning to this new and wondrously rowdy Arab. Already it was quite evident that she was not indifferent to him. Fortunately Ahmed came in time to shoot Omair before Diana's Unconscious could flash to her any realization of a new love.

And the book does end happily, even more happily than anybody has a right to expect. Ahmed is badly wounded but only in the head, and recovers without any impairment of his punching power. The greatest surprise of all is reserved for the last chapter, when Diana and the reader learn that Ben isn't really an Arab at all, but the eldest son of Lord Glencaryll, and of Lady Glencaryll, too, for that matter. It seems Lord Glencaryll drank excessively, although his title was one of the oldest in England. Lady Glencaryll left him on account of his alcoholism and went to the Sahara desert for rest and contrast. A courtly sheik gave her shelter in his oasis. Here her son was born, and when he heard about his father's disgraceful conduct he turned Arab and stayed that way. Of course, if he had intended nothing more than a protest against overindulgence in alcoholic liquors he could have turned American. We suppose such a device would not have seemed altogether plausible. No Englishman could pass for an American. Nor can we say that we are altogether satisfied with the ending even as it stands. For all we know E. M. Hull may decide to take a shot at Uncle Tom's Cabin and add a chapter revealing the fact that Uncle Tom was not actually a colored man but the child of a couple of Caucasians who had happened to get a little sunburned. We are not even sure that E. M. Hull is a woman. Publishers do get fooled about such things. According to our theory, the E stands for Egbert. He is, we think, at least five feet four inches tall and lives in Bloomsbury, in very respectable bachelor diggings. He has never been to the desert or near it, but if "The Sheik" continues to run through new editions he plans to take a jaunt to the East. He thinks it might help his hay fever.

II

In the course of his Sabbath day talk at Calvary
Baptist Church the other day the Rev. Dr. John
Roach Straton spoke of "miserable Charlie Chaplin,"
or words to that effect. This seems to us an expression of the more or less natural antipathy of a man
who regards life trivially for a serious artist. It is
the venom of the clown confronted by the comedian.

Dr. Straton is, of course, an utter materialist. He
is concerned with such temporal and evanescent
things as hellfire, and a heaven which he has pictured
in one of his sermons as a sort of glorified Coney
Island. Moreover, he has created a deity in his own
image and has presented the invisible king as merely
a somewhat more mannerly John Roach Straton. And
while Dr. Straton has been thus engaged in debasing
the ideals of mankind, Charlie Chaplin has brought
to great masses of people some glint of things which
are eternal. He has managed to show us beauty and,
better than that, he has contrived to put us at ease in
this presence. We belong to a Nation which is timorous of beauty, but Charlie has managed to soothe
our fears by proving to us that it may also be merry.

While Straton has been talking about jazz, de-
bauchery, modesty, vengeance and other ugly things,

23

Chaplin has given us the story of a child. "The Kid" captured a little of that curiously exalted something which belongs to paternity. All spiritual things must have in them a childlike quality. The belief in immortality rests not very much on the hope of going on. Few of us want to do that, but we would like very much to begin again.

Naturally, we are under no delusions as to the innate goodness even of very small children. They are bad a great deal of the time, but before it has been knocked out of them they see no limit to the potentialities of the human will. Theirs is the faith to move mountains, because they do not yet know the fearful heft of them. The world is merely a rather big sandpile and much may be done to it with a tin pail and shovel. We would capture such confidence again.

As a matter of fact, a great deal could be done with a pail and shovel. We do not try because we have lost our nerve. Nobody will ever get it back again by listening to Dr. Straton. He seems solely intent upon detailing the limitations and the frailties of man. We think he has outgrown his soul a little. He has sold his birthright for a mess of potterism.

But Charlie Chaplin moves through the world which he pictures on the screen like a mischievous child. He confounds all the gross villains who come against him. His smile is a token and a symbol that man is too merry to die utterly. Fearful things menace us, but they will flee before the audacious one who has the fervor to draw back his foot and let it fly.

Of course, we are not advocating any suppression
24

of Dr. Straton by censorship. We regard him and his sermons as a bad influence. But after all, the man or woman who strays into Dr. Straton's church knows what to expect. In justice to the clergyman it must be said that he has never made any secret of his methods or his message. There is no deception. Sentimentally, we think it rather shocking that these talks of his should occur on Sunday. There really ought to be one day of the week upon which the citizens of New York turn away from frivolity. And still we do not urge that the Sunday Law be amended to include the performances of John Roach Straton. He is not one whit worse than some of the sensational Sunday magazines.

III

PRIVATE OWNERSHIP OF OFFSPRING

Fannie Hurst gurgles with joy over the fact that her heroine in "Star Dust" is able to look over the whole tray of babies which is brought to her in the hospital and pick out her own. Miss Hurst attributes Lily's feat to "her mother instinct." A friend of ours, more practically minded than the novelist, suggests that she might have been aided by the fact that hospitals invariably place an identification tag around the neck of each child. For our part we have never been able to understand the fear of some parents about babies getting mixed up in the hospital. What difference does it make so long as you get a good one? Another's may be better than your own and Lily, with a whole tray from which to choose, should not have made an instinctive clutch immmediately for her own. It would have been rational for the lady in the story to have looked at them all before coming to any decision.

Of course, to tell the truth, there isn't much choice in the little ones. They need much more than necklaces with names on them to be persons. There really ought to be some system whereby small children after being born could be kept in the shop for a considerable period, like puppies, and not turned over to parents or guardians until in a condition more disciplined than usual. None of them amounts to much during the first year. We can't see, for the life of us, why your own should be any more interesting or precious to you during this time than the child of anybody else.

After two, of course, they are persons, but a parent must have a good deal of imagination if he can see much of himself in a child. Oh, yes, a nose or the eyes or the color of the hair or something like that, but the world is full of snub noses and brown eyes. To us it never seemed much more than a coincidence. And if it were something more, what of it? How can a man work up any inspiring sentimental gratification over the fact that after he is gone his nose will persist in the world? The hope of immortality through offspring offers no solace to us. The joys of being an ancestor are exaggerated.

Mind you, we do not mean for a moment to cry down the undeniable pleasure which arises from the privilege of being associated with a child of more than two years of age. For a person in rugged health who is not particularly dressed up and does not want to write a letter or read the newspaper, we can imagine few diversions more enjoyable than to have a child turned loose upon him. His own, if you wish, but only in the sense that it is the one to which he has become accustomed. The sense of paternity has nothing on earth to do with the fun. Only a person extraordinarily satisfied with himself can derive pleasure if this child in his house is a little person who gives him back nothing but a reflection. You want a new story and not the old one, which wasn't particularly satisfactory in the first place. We want Heywood Broun, 3rd, to start from scratch without having to lug along anything we have left him. As a matter of fact, we like him just as well as if he were no relation at all, because he seeems to be a person quite different from what we might have expected. When he says he doesn't want to take a bath we feel abashed and wish we had been a cleaner child, but for the most part we find him leading his own life altogether. When he bends over the Victrola and plays the Siegfried Funeral March over and over again we have no feeling of guilt. We know we can't be blamed for that. He never got it from us.

And again, he is a person utterly strange, and therefore twice as interesting, when we find him standing up to people, us for instance, and saying that he won't do this or that because he doesn't want to. Much sharper than a serpent's tooth is the pleasure of an abject parent who finds himself the father of a stubborn child. If the people from the hospital should suddenly call up to-morrow and say, "We find we've made a mistake. We sent the wrong child to you three years ago, but now we can exchange him and rectify everything," we would say, "No, this one's been around quite a while now and is giving approximate satisfaction, and if you don't mind you can keep the real one."

Plays and novels which picture meetings between fathers and sons parted from birth or before have always seemed singularly unconvincing to us. The

28

old man says "My boy! My boy!" and weeps, and the young man looks him warmly in the eye and says, "There, there." Not a bit like it is our guess. If we had never seen H, 3rd, and had then met him at the end of twenty years, we wouldn't be particularly interested. Strangers always embarrass us. It would not even shock us much to find that they had sent him to Yale or that he brushed his hair straight back or wore spats. There are to us no ties at all just in being a father. A son is distinctly an acquired taste. It's the practice of parenthood that makes you feel that, after all, there may be something in it. And anybody's child will do for practice.

IV

The ship news man said that Gilbert K. Chesterton
was staying at the Commodore and the telephone girl
said he wasn't, but we'd trust even a ship news man
before a hotel central and so we persisted.

In fact, we almost persuaded her.

"Maybe he's connected with one of the automobile
companies that are exhibiting here," she suggested,
helpfully. For a moment we wondered if by any
chance the hotel authorities had made an error and
placed him in the lobby with the ten-ton trucks. It
seemed too fantastic.

"He's not with any automobile company," we
said severely. "Didn't you ever hear of 'The Man
Who Was Thursday'?"

"He may have been here Thursday, but he's not
registered now," she answered with some assurance.
We didn't seem to be getting on. "It's a book," we
shouted. "He wrote it."

"Not in this hotel," said central with an air of
finality and rang off before we could try her out on
"Man Alive" or "The Ball and the Cross." Still, it
turned out eventually that she was right for it was
the Biltmore which at last acknowledged Mr. Chester-

ton somewhat reluctantly after we had spelled out the name.

"Not in his room, but somewhere about the hotel," was the message.

"You can find him," said the city editor with confidence. "Just take this picture with you. He's sort of fat and he speaks with an English accent."

We had a more helpful description than that in our mind, because we remembered Chesterton's answer when a sweet girl admirer once remarked, "It must be wonderful to walk .along the streets when everybody knows who you are."

"Yes," said Chesterton; "and if they don't know they ask."

He wasn't in the bar, but we found him in the smoking room. He was giving somebody an interview without much enthusiasm. It seemed to be the last round. Chesterton was beginning to droop. Every paradox, we feared, had beeen hammered out of him. He rose a little wearily and started for the elevator. We chased him. At last we had the satisfaction of finding some one we could outrun. He paused, and now we know the look which the Wedding Guest must have given to the Ancient Mariner.

"It's for the New York *Tribune*," we said."

"How about next week?" suggested Mr. Chesterton.

"It's a daily newspaper," we remonstrated. "You know—Grantland Rice and The Conning Tower and When a Feller Needs a Friend."

Something in the title of the Briggs series must have touched him. "To-morrow, perhaps," he answered. Feeling that the mountain was about to come through we stood our ground like another Mahomet. Better than that we rose to one of the few superb moments in our life. Looking at Mr. Chesterton coldly we said slowly, "It must be now or never." And we used a gesture. The nature of it escapes us, but it was something appropriate. Later we wondered just what reply would have been possible if he had answered, "Never." After the danger had passed we realized that we had been holding up the visitor with an empty gun. It must have been our manner which awed him and he stopped walking and almost turned around.

"The press men have been here since two o'clock," he complained more in sorrow than in anger. "What is it you want to know?"

At that stage of the interview the advantage passed to him. The whole world lay before us. Dimly we could hear the problems of a great and unhappy universe flapping in our ears and urging us with unintelligible, hoarse caws to present their cases for solution. And still we stood there unable to think of a single thing which we wanted to know.

Mostly we had read Chesterton on rum and religion, but there were too many people passing to give the proper atmosphere for any such confidential questions. Moreover, if he should question us in turn we realized that we would be unable to give him any information as to when to boil and when to skim, nor did we feel sufficiently well disposed to let him in on the name of the drug store where you say "I'm a patient of Dr. Brown's" and are forthwith allowed to buy gin.

32

G. K. C.

All the questions we had ever asked anybody in our life passed rapidly before us. "What do you think of our tall buildings?" "Have you ever thought of playing Hamlet?" "Why are you called the woman with the most beautiful legs in Paris?" We remembered that the last had seemed silly even when we first used it on Mistinguett. On second thought we had told the interpreter to let it drop because the photographers were anxious to begin. There seemed to be even less sense to it now. Indeed none of our familiar inquiries struck us as appropriate.

"What American authors do you read?" we ventured timidly, and added "living ones" hoping to get something about "Main Street" for Wednesday's book column.

"I don't read any," he answered.

That seemed to us a possible handicap in pursuing that line of inquiry.

"I don't read any living English authors, either," Mr. Chesterton added hastily, as if he feared that he had trod upon our patriotism. "Nothing but dead authors and detective stories."

That we had expected. In the march up to the heights of fame there comes a spot close to the summit in which man reads "nothing but detective stories." It is the Antæan touch which distinguishes all Olympians. As you remember, Antæus was the demigod who had to touch the earth every once and so often to preserve his immortality. Probably he did it by reading a good murder story.

"Can you tell me what 'Mary Rose' is all about?" we suggested, still fumbling for a literary theme.

"I haven't seen 'Mary Rose,' " said Mr. Chesterton, although he did go on to tell us that Barrie had done several excellent plays. Probably there was a long pause then while we tried to think up something provocative about the Irish question.

"If you really will excuse me, I must go to my room," he burst out. "The press men have been here ever since two o'clock."

This, of course, is no land in which to stand between a man and his room, where heaven knows what solace may await the distinguished visitor who has been spending two and a half hours with the press men. We stepped aside willingly enough. Still, we must confess a slight disappointment in Gilbert K. Chesterton. He's not as fat as we had heard.

V

ON BEING A GOD

We have found a way to feel very close kin to the high gods. The notion that we too leaned out from the gold bar of heaven came to us suddenly as we sat in the right field bleachers of one of the big theaters which provide a combination bill of vaudeville and motion pictures. The process of deification occurred during the vaudeville portion of the program.

The stage was several miles away. We could see perfectly and hear nothing as it was said. Curious little, insect-like people moved about the stage aimlessly. And yet there was every evidence that they took themselves seriously. You would be surprised if you watched ants conducting a performance and calling for light cues and such things. It would puzzle you to know why one particular ant took care to provide himself with a flood of red and another just as arbitrarily chose green.

Still, these were not ants but potentially men and women. They had names—Kerrigan and Vane, the Kaufman Trio, Miss Minstrel Co. and many others. From where we sat they were insects. It seemed to us that it would be no trouble at all to flip the three strong men and the pony ballet into oblivion with one

35

finger. The little finger would be the most suitable.

And there were times when we wanted to do it. Only, the feeling that we were too new a god to impose a doom restrained us. No divine patience was in us, but we felt that if we could wait a while it might come. The agitated atoms annoyed us. The audacity of "pony ballet" was almost insufferable. Why, as in Gulliver's land, the biggest of the strong men towered above the smallest of the ballet girls by at least the thickness of a fingernail. And these performing ants were forever working to entertain. They ran on and off the stage without apparent reason and waved their antennæ about furiously. Two of the ants would stand close together as if in conversation, and every now and then one of them would hit the other brutally in the face.

We did not know why and our sympathies went entirely to the one who was struck. It was difficult not to interfere. We rather think that some of the seemingly extraordinary judgments of the high gods between mortals must be explained on the ground of a somewhat similar imperfect knowledge. They too see us, but they cannot hear. Time is required for sound to reach Olympus. When we get into warfare they observe only the carnage and the turmoil. The preliminary explanations arrive several years after the peace treaties have been signed, and then they sound silly and entirely irrelevant.

Accordingly, the high gods are rather loath to interfere in the wars of earth. They are too far removed to understand causes, and even trumpet-like shouts about national honor merely amble up to their ears through long lanes of retarding ether. Indeed, the period of transit is so long that national honor invariably arrives at Olympus in poor condition. Only when strictly fresh is it in the least inspiring. Little old last century's national honor is quite unpalatable. It is food neither for gods nor men.

It was just as well that we waited before taking blind vengeance on the vaudeville insects, because half an hour or so after the blows were struck by the seemingly aggressive ant the conversation which preceded the violence began to drift back to us. It came to our ears during the turn of the strong men and created a rather uncanny effect. At first we were puzzled because we had never known strong men to exchange any words at all except the traditional "alleyup." Almost immediately we realized that it was merely the tardiness of sound waves which caused the delay of the dialogue in reaching us in our bleacher seat.

Fortunately, in spite of our illusion of omnipotence, the distance from the stage was not truly Olympian. The jokes came in time to be appreciated. It seems that one of the ants, whom we shall immediately christen A, told his friend and companion, B for convenience, that he was taking two ladies to dinner and that he would like to have B in the party, but that he, A, did not have sufficient funds to defray any expense which he might incur. B admitted promptly that he himself had nothing. Accordingly, A suggested a scheme for sociability's sake. He urged B to come, but impressed upon him that

37

when asked as to what he wished to eat or drink he should reply, "I don't care for anything."

In order to guard against a slip-up the friendly ants rehearsed the scene in advance. It ran something like this:

A—August! August!

B—You're a little wrong on your months. This is January.

A (punching him)—You fool! August is the name of the waiter.

The delay which retarded the progress of this joke to our ears impaired its effectiveness a little. The rest was more sprightly.

A—August, bring some chicken en casserole and combination salad for myself and the two ladies. Oh, I've forgotten my friend. What will you have?

B—Bring me some pigs' knuckles.

At this point A hit B for the second time and again called him a fool.

A—Why did you say, "Bring me some pigs' knuckles?"

B—Why did you ask me so pretty?

Thereupon they rehearsed the situation again.

A—Oh, I've forgotten my friend. Won't you have something? You must join us.

B—Sure, bring me a dish of ham and eggs.

Again blows were struck and again A inquired ferociously as to the cause of the slip-up.

A—What made you say, "Bring me a dish of ham and eggs?"

B—Well, why did you go and coax me?

Earlier in the evening we had observed that other

38

blows were struck and there must have been further dialogue to go with them, but we could not wait for it to arrive. We rather hoped that the jokes would follow us home, but they must have become lost on the way.

Perhaps you don't think there was much sense to this talk anyway.

Maybe the real gods on high Olympus feel the same way about us when our words limp home.

VI

CHIVALRY IS BORN

Every now and then we hear parents commenting on the fearful things which motion pictures may do to the minds of children. They seem to think that a little child is full of sweetness and of light. We had the same notion until we had a chance to listen intently to the prattle of a three-year-old. Now we know that no picture can possibly outdo him in his own fictionized frightfulness.

Of course, we had heard testimony to this effect from Freudians, but we had supposed that all these horrible blood lusts and such like were suppressed. Unfortunately, our own son is without reticence. We have a notion that each individual goes through approximately the same stages of progress as the race. Heywood Broun, 3d, seemed not yet quite as high as the cavemen in his concepts. For the last few months he has been harping continuously, and chiefly during meal times, about cutting off people's noses and gouging out eyes. In his range of speculative depredations he has invariably seemed liberal.

There seemed to us, then, no reason to fear that new notions of horror would come to Heywood Broun, 3d, from any of the pictures being licensed at present in this State. As a matter of fact, he has received from the films his first notions of chivalry. Of course, we are not at all sure that this is beneficial. We like his sentimentalism a little worse than his sadism.

After seeing "Tol'able David," for instance, we had a long argument. Since our experience with motion pictures is longer than his we often feel reasonably certain that our interpretation of the happenings is correct and we do not hesitate to contradict H. 3d, although he is so positive that sometimes our confidence is shaken. We knew that he was all wrong about "Tol'able David" because it was quite evident that he had become mixed in his mind concerning the hero and the villain. He kept insisting that David was a bad man because he fought. Pacifism has always seemed to us an appealing philosophy, but it came with bad grace from such a swashbuckling disciple of frightfulness as H. 3d.

However, we did not develop that line of reasoning but contended that David had to fight in order to protect himself. Woodie considered this for a while and then answered triumphantly, "David hit a woman."

Our disgust was unbounded. Film life had seared the child after all. Actually, it was not David who hit the woman but the villainous Luke Hatburn, the terrible mountaineer. That error in observation was not the cause of our worry. The thing that bothered us was that here was a young individual, not yet four years of age, who was already beginning to talk in terms of "the weaker vessel" and all the other phrases

41

of a romantic school we believed to be dying. It could not have shocked us more if he had said, "Woman's place is in the home."

"David hit a woman," he piped again, seeming to sense our consternation. "What of it?" we cried, but there was no bullying him out of his point of view. The fault belongs entirely to the motion pictures. H. 3d cannot truthfully say that he has had the slightest hint from us as to any sex inferiority of women. By word and deed we have tried to set him quite the opposite example. We have never allowed him to detect us for an instant in any chivalrous act or piece of partial sex politeness. Toasts such as "The ladies, God bless 'em" are not drunk in our house, nor has Woodie ever heard "Shall we join the ladies," "the fair sex," "the weaker sex," or any other piece of patronizing masculine poppycock. Susan B. Anthony's picture hangs in his bedroom side by side with Abraham Lincoln and the big elephant. He has led a sheltered life and has never been allowed to play with nice children.

But, somehow or other, chivalry and romanticism creep into each life even through barred windows. We have no intention of being too hard upon the motion pictures. Something else would have introduced it. These phases belong in the development of the race. H. 3d must serve his time as gentle knight just as he did his stint in the rôle of sadistic caveman. Presently, we fear, he will get to the crusades and we shall suffer during a period in which he will try to improve our manners. History will then be our only consolation. We shall try to bear up secure in the knowledge that the dark ages are still ahead of him.

We hoped that the motion pictures might be used as an antidote against the damage which they had done. We took H. 3d to see Nazimova in "A Doll's House." There was a chance, we thought, that he might be moved by the eloquent presentation of the fact that before all else a woman is a human being and just as eligible to be hit as anybody else. We read him the caption embodying Nora's defiance, but at the moment it flashed upon the screen he had crawled under his seat to pick up an old program and the. words seemed to have no effect. Indeed when Nora went out into the night, slamming the door behind her, he merely hazarded that she was "going to Mr. Butler's." Mr. Butler happens to be our grocer.

The misapprehension was not the fault of Nazimova. She flung herself out of the house magnificently, but Heywood Broun, 3d, insisted on believing that she had gone around the corner for a dozen eggs.

In discussing the picture later, we found that he had quite missed the point of Mr. Ibsen's play. Of Nora, the human being, he remembered nothing. It was only Nora, the mother, who had impressed him. All he could tell us about the great and stimulating play was that the lady had crawled on the floor with her little boy and her little girl. And yet it seems to us that Ibsen has told his story with singular clarity.

D'Artagnan Woodie likes very much. He is fond of recalling to our mind the fact that D'Artagnan

43

"walked on the roof in his nightshirt." H. 3d is not allowed on the roof nor is he permitted to wander about in his nightshirt.

Perhaps the child's introduction to the films has been somewhat too haphazard. As we remember, the first picture which we saw together was called "Is Life Worth Living?" The worst of it is that circumstances made it necessary for us to leave before the end and so neither of us found out the answer.

VII

We picked up "Who's Who in America" yesterday to get some vital statistics about Babe Ruth, and found to our surprise that he was not in the book. Even as George Herman Ruth there is no mention of him. The nearest name we could find was: "Roth, Filibert, forestry expert; b. Wurttemberg, Germany, April 20, 1858; s. Paul Raphael and Amalie (Volz) R., early edn. in Württemberg——"

There is in our heart not an atom of malice against Prof. Roth (since September, 1903, he has been "prof. forestry, U. Mich."), and yet we question the justice of his admission to a list of national celebrities while Ruth stands without. We know, of course, that Prof. Roth is the author of "Forest Conditions in Wisconsin" and of "The Uses of Wood," but we wonder whether he has been able to describe in words uses of wood more sensational and vital than those which Ruth has shown in deeds. Hereby we challenge the editor of "Who's Who in America" to debate the affirmative side of the question: Resolved, That Prof. Roth's volume called "Timber Physics" has exerted a more profound influence in the life of America than Babe Ruth's 1921 home-run record.

The question is, of course, merely a continuation

45

of the ancient controversy as to the relative importance of the theorist and the practitioner; should history prefer in honor the man who first developed the hypothesis that the world was round or the other who went out and circumnavigated it? What do we owe to Ben Franklin and what to the lightning? Shall we celebrate Newton or the apple?

Personally, our sympathies go out to the performer rather than the fellow in the study or the laboratory. Many scientists staked their reputations on the fact that the world was round before Magellan set sail in the *Vittoria*. He did not lack written assurances that there was no truth in the old tale of a flat earth with dragons and monsters lurking just beyond the edges.

But suppose, in spite of all this, Magellan had gone on sailing, sailing until his ship did topple over into the void of dragons and big snakes. The professors would have been abashed. Undoubtedly they would have tried to laugh the misfortune off, and they might even have been good enough sports to say, "That's a fine joke on us." But at worst they could lose nothing but their reputations, which can be made over again. Magellan would not live to profit by his experience. Being one of those foreigners, he had no sense of humor, and if the dragons bit him as he fell, it is ten to one he could not even manage to smile.

By this time we have rather traveled away from Roth's "Timber Physics" and Ruth's home-run record, but we hope that you get what we mean. Without knowing the exact nature of "Timber Physics," we assume that the professor discusses the most efficient manner in which to bring about the greatest possible impact between any wooden substance and a given object. But mind you, he merely discusses it. If the professor chances to be wrong, even if he is wrong three times, nobody in the classroom is likely to poke a sudden finger high in the air and shout, "You're out!"

The professor remains at bat during good behavior. He is not subject to any such sudden vicissitudes as Ruth. Moreover, timber physics is to Mr. Roth a matter of cool and calm deliberation. No adversary seeks to fool him with speed or spitballs. "Hit it out" never rings in his ears. And after all, just what difference does it make if Mr. Roth errs in his timber physics? It merely means that a certain number of students leave Michigan knowing a little less than they should—and nobody expects anything else from students.

On the other hand, a miscalculation by Ruth in the uses of wood affects much more important matters. A strike-out on his part may bring about complete tragedy and the direst misfortune. There have been occasions, and we fear that there will still be occasions, when Ruth's bat will be the only thing which stands between us and the loss of the American League pennant. In times like these who cares about "Forest Conditions in Wisconsin"?

Coming to the final summing up for our side of the question at debate, we shall try to lift the whole affair above any mere Ruth versus Roth issue. It will be our endeavor to show that not only has Babe Ruth been a profound interest and influence in America, but that on the whole he has been a power for progress. Ruth has helped to make life a little more gallant. He has set before us an example of a man who tries each minute for all or nothing. When he is not knocking home runs he is generally striking out, and isn't there more glory in fanning in an effort to put the ball over the fence than in prolonging a little life by playing safe?

48

VIII

THE BIGGER THE YEAR

As soon as we heard that "The Big Year—A College Story" by Meade Minnigerode was about Yale we knew that we just had to read it. Tales of travel and curious native customs have always fascinated us. According to Mr. Minnigerode the men of Yale walk about their campus in big blue sweaters with "Y's" on them, smoking pipes and singing college songs under the windows of one another. The seniors, he informs us, come out on summer afternoons on roller skates.

Of course, we are disposed to believe that Mr. Minnigerode, like all travelers in strange lands, is prone to color things a little more highly than exact accuracy would sanction. We felt this particularly when he began to write about Yale football. There was, for instance, Curly Corliss, the captain of the eleven, who is described as "starting off after a punt to tear back through a broken field, thirty and forty yards at a clip, tackling an opposing back with a deadliness which was final—never hurt, always smiling—a blond head of curly hair (he never wore a headguard) flashing in and out across the field, the hands clapping together, the plaintive voice calling 'All right, all right, give me the ball!' when a game

49

was going badly, and then carrying it alone to touchdown after touchdown."

Although we have seen all of Yale's recent big games we recognized none of that except "the plaintive voice" and even that would have been more familiar if it had been used to say "Moral victory!" We waited to find Mr. Minnigerode explaining that of course he was referring to the annual contest with the Springfield Training School, but he did no such thing and went straight ahead with the pretense that football at Yale is romantic. To be sure, he attempts to justify this attitude by letting us see a good deal of the gridiron doings through the eyes of a bull terrier who could not well be expected to be captious. Champ, named after the Yale chess team, came by accident to the field just as Curly Corliss was off on one of his long runs. Yes, it was a game against the scrubs. "Some one came tearing along and lunged at Curly as he went by, apparently trying to grab him about the legs. Champ cast all caution to the winds. Interfere with Curly, would he? Well, Champ guessed not! Like an arrow from a bow Champ hurled himself through the air and fastened his jaws firmly in the seat of the offender's pants, in a desperate effort to prevent him from further molesting Curly."

Champ was immediately adopted by the team as mascot. It seems to us he deserved more, for this was the first decent piece of interference seen on Yale field in years. The associate mascot was Jimmy, a little newsboy, who also took football at New Haven seriously. His romanticism, like that of Champ, was understandable. Hadn't Curly Corliss once saved his life? We need not tell you that he had. "Jimmy," as Mr. Minnigerode tells the story, "started to run across the street, without noticing the street-car lumbering around the corner . . . and then before he knew it Jimmy tripped and fell, and the car was almost on top of him grinding its brakes. Jimmy never knew exactly what happened in the next few seconds, but he heard people shouting, and then something struck him and he was dragged violently away by the seat of the pants. When he could think connectedly again he was sitting on the curb considerably battered—and Curly was sitting beside him, with his trousers torn, nursing a badly cut hand."

We remember there was an incident like that in Cambridge once, only the man who rescued the newsboy was not the football captain but a substitute on the second team. We have forgotten his name. Unlike Corliss of Yale, the Harvard man did not bother to pick up the newsboy. Instead he seized the street car and threw it for a loss.

.   .   .   .   .   .

The first half was over and Princeton led by a score of 10 to 0. Things looked blue for Yale. Neither mascot was on hand. Yale was trying to win with nothing but students. Where was little Jimmy the newsboy? If you must know he was in the hospital, for he had been run over again. The boy could not seem to break himself of the habit. Unfortunately he had picked out the afternoon of the Princeton game when all the Yale players were much too busy trying to stop Tigers to have any time to

51

interfere with traffic. It was only an automobile this time and Jimmy escaped with a mere gash over one eye. Champ, the bull terrier who caused the mixup, was uninjured. "I'm all right now," Jimmy told the doctor, "honest I am—can I go—I gotta take Champ out to the game—he's the mascot and they can't win without him—please, Mister, let me go—I guess they need us bad out there."

Apparently the crying need of Yale football is not so much a coaching system as a good leash to keep the mascots from getting run over. Champ and Jimmy rushed into the locker room just as the big Blue team was about to trot out for the second half. After that there was nothing to it. Yale won by a score of 12 to 10. "Curly clapped his hands together," writes Mr. Minnegerode in describing the rally, "and kept calling out 'Never mind the signal! Give me the ball' in his plaintive voice"——

This sounds more like Yale football than anything else in the book. However, it sufficed. Curly made two touchdowns and all the Yale men went to Mory's and sang "Curly Corliss, Curly Corliss, he will leave old Harvard scoreless." It is said that a legend is now gaining ground in New Haven that Yale will not defeat Harvard again until it is led by some other captain whose name rhymes with "scoreless." The current captain of the Elis is named Jordan. The only thing that rhymes with is "scored on."

Still, as Professor Billy Phelps has taught his students to say, football isn't everything. Perhaps something of Sparta has gone from Yale, for a few years or forever, but just look at the Yale poets and novelists all over the place. There is a new kindliness at New Haven. Take for instance the testimony of the same "Big Year" when it describes a touching little scene between Curly Corliss, the captain of the Yale football team, and his room mate as they are revealed in the act of retiring for the night:

" 'Angel!'

" 'Yeah,' very sleepily.

" 'They all seem to get over it!'

" 'Over what?'

" 'The follows who have graduated,' Curly explained. 'I guess they all feel pretty poor when they leave, but they get over it right away. It's just like changing into a new suit, I expect.'

" 'Yeah, I guess so' . . .

" 'Well, goo' night, little feller' . . .

" 'Goo' night, Teddy.' "

But we do wish Mr. Minnegerode had been a little more explicit and had told us who tucked them in.

IX

FOR OLD NASSAU

Wadsworth Camp, we find, has done almost as much for Princeton in his novel, "The Guarded Heights," as Meade Minnigerode has accomplished for Yale in "The Big Year."

George Morton might never have gone to any college if it had not been for Sylvia Planter. He was enamored of her from the very beginning when old Planter engaged him to accompany his daughter on rides, but his admiration did not become articulate until she fell off her horse. She seems to have done it extremely well. "He saw her horse refuse," writes Mr. Camp, "straightening his knees and sliding in the marshy ground. He watched Sylvia, with an ease and grace nearly unbelievable, somersault across the hedge and out of sight in the meadow beyond."

It seemed to us that the horse should have received some of the credit for the ease with which Sylvia shot across the hedge, but young Morton was much too intent upon the fate of his goddess to have eyes for anything else. When he found her lying on the ground she was unconscious, and so he told her of his love. That brought her to and she called him "You—you—stable boy." And so George decided to go to college.

54

His high school preparation had been scant and irregular. He went to Princeton, and after two months' cramming passed all his examinations. Football attracted him from the first as a means to the advancement which he desired. "With surprised eyes," writes our author, "he saw estates as extravagant as Oakmont, and frequently in better taste. Little by little he picked up the names of the families that owned them. He told himself that some day he would enter those places as a guest, bowed to by such servants as he had been. It was possible, he promised himself bravely, if only he could win a Yale or a Harvard game."

Perhaps this explains why one meets so few Princeton men socially. Some, we have found, are occasionally invited to drop in after dinner. These, we assume, are recruited from the ranks of those Princetonians who have tied Yale or Harvard or at least held the score down.

Like Mr. Minnigerode, Mr. Camp employs symbolism in his story. In the Yale novel we had Corliss evidently standing for Coy. Just which Princeton hero George Morton represents we are not prepared to say. In fact, the only Princeton name which comes to mind at the moment is that of Big Bill Edwards who used to sit in the Customs House and throw them all for a loss. Morton can hardly be intended for Edwards because it seems unlikely that anybody would ever have engaged Big Bill to ride horses; no, not even to break them. A little further on, however, we are introduced to the Princeton coach, a certain Mr. Stringham. Here, to be sure,

identification is easy. Stringham, we haven't a doubt,
is Roper. We could wish Mr. Camp had been more
subtle. He might, for instance, have called him Cor-
dier.

In some respects Morton proved an even better football player than Corliss. He did not score any greater
number of touchdowns, but he had more of an air
with him. Thus, in the account of the Harvard game
it is recorded: "Then, with his interference blocked
and tumbling, George yielded to his old habit and
slipped off to one side at a hazard. The enemy's
secondary defense had been drawing in, there was no
one near enough to stop him within those ten yards
and he went over for a touchdown and casually
kicked the goal."

Eventually, George Morton did get asked to all
the better houses, but still Sylvia spurned him. "Go
away and don't bother me," was the usual form of
her replies to his ardent words of wooing. Naturally
he knew that he had her on the run. A man who
had taken more than one straight arm squarely in
the face during the course of his football career was
not to be rebuffed by a slip of a girl.

The war delayed matters for a time, and George
went and was good at that too. He was a major before he left Plattsburgh. For a time we feared that
he was in danger of becoming a snob, but the great
democratizing forces of the conflict carried him into
the current. One of the most thrilling chapters in
the book tells how he exposed his life under very
heavy fire to go forward and rescue an American
who turned out to be a Yale man.

FOR OLD NASSAU

There was no stopping George Morton. In the end he wore Sylvia down. Nothing else could be expected from such a man. German machine guns and heavy artillery had failed to stop him and he had even hit the Harvard line, upon occasion, without losing a yard.

His head was hard and he could not take a hint. In the end Sylvia just had to marry him. Her right hand swing was not good enough. "As in a dream he went to her, and her curved lips moved beneath his, but he pressed them closer so that she couldn't speak; for he felt encircling them in a breathless embrace, as his arms held her, something thrilling and rudimentary that neither of them had experienced before——"

And as we read the further details of the love scene it seemed to us that George Morton had made a most fortunate choice when he decided to go to Princeton. His football experience stood him in good stead in his love-making, for he had been trained with an eleven which tackled around the neck.

X

MR. DEMPSEY'S FIVE-FOOT SHELF

It is hardly fair to expect Jack Dempsey to take literature very seriously. How, for instance, can he afford to pay much attention to George Bernard Shaw who declared just before the fight that Carpentier could not lose and ought to be quoted at odds of fifty to one? From the point of view of Dempsey, then, creative evolution, the superman and all the rest, are the merest moonshine. He might well take the position that since Mr. Shaw was so palpably wrong about the outcome of the fight two days before it happened, it scarcely behooves anybody to pay much attention to his predictions as to the fate of the world and mankind two thousand years hence.

Whatever the reason, Jack Dempsey does not read George Bernard Shaw much. But he has heard of him. When some reporter came to Dempsey a day or so before the fight and told him that Shaw had fixed fifty to one as the proper odds on Carpentier, the champion made no comment. The newspaper gossiper, disappointed of his sensation, asked if Dempsey had ever heard of Shaw and the fighter stoutly maintained that he had. The examination went no further but it is fair to assume that Dempsey did know the great British sporting writer. It was not remarkable that he paid no attention to his prediction. Dempsey would not even be moved much by a prediction from Hughie Fullerton.

In other words literature and life are things divorced in Dempsey's mind. He does read. The first time we ever saw Dempsey he discussed books with not a little interest. He was not at his training quarters when we arrived but his press agent showed us about—a singularly reverential man this press agent. "This," he said, and he seemed to lower his voice, "is the bed where Jack Dempsey sleeps." All the Louises knew better beds and so did Lafayette even when a stranger in a strange land. Washington himself fared better in the midst of war. Nor can it be said that there was anything very compelling about the room in which Dempsey slept. It had air but not much distinction. There were just two pictures on the wall. One represented a heavy surf upon an indeterminate but rather rockbound coast and the other showed a lady asleep with cupids hovering about her bed. Although the thought is erotic the artist had removed all that in the execution.

Much more striking was the fact that upon a chair beside the bed of Dempsey lay a couple of books and a magazine. It was not *The Bookman* but *Photo Play*. The books were "The Czar's Spy" by William Le Queux, "The Spoilers" by Rex Beach, and at least one other Western novel which we have unfortunately forgotten. It was, as we remember it, the Luck of the Lazy Something or Other. The press agent said that Jack read quite a little and pointed to the reading light which had been strung over his bed.

He then went on to show us the clothes closet and the bureau of the champion to prove that he was no slave to fashion. We can testify that only one pair of shoes in the room had gray suede tops. Then we saw the kitchen and were done.

There had been awe in the tones of the conductor from the beginning. "Jack's going to have roast lamb for dinner to-night," he announced in an awful hush. Even as we went out he could not resist lowering his voice a little as he said, "This is the hat rack. This is where the champion puts his hat." We had gone only fifty yards away from the house when a big brown limousine drew up. "That," said the press agent, and this time we feared he was going to die, "is Jack Dempsey himself."

The preparation had been so similar to the first act of "Enter Madame" that we expected temperament and gesture from the star. He put us wholly at ease by being much more frightened than any one in the visiting party. As somebody has said somewhere, "Any mouse can make this elephant squeal." Jack Dempsey is decidedly a timid man and we found later that he was a gentle one. He answered, "Yes, sir," and "No, sir," at first. If we had his back and shoulders we'd have a civil word for no man. By and by he grew a little more at ease and somebody asked him what he read. He was not particularly strong on the names of books and he always forgot the author, which detracts somewhat from this article as a guide for readers. There were almost three hundred books at his disposal, since his training quarters had once been an aviation camp. These were the books of the fliers. Practically all the popular novelists and short story writers were represented. We remember seeing several titles by Mary Roberts Rinehart, Irvin Cobb, Zane Grey, Rupert Hughes, and Rex Beach. Older books were scarce. The only one we noticed was "A Tale of Two Cities." This Dempsey had not read. Perhaps Jack Kearns advised against it on account of the possible disturbing psychological effects of the chapter with all the counting.

Dempsey said he had devoted most of his time to Western novels. When questioned he admitted that he did not altogether surrender himself to them. "I was a cowboy once for a while," he said. "There's a lot of hokum in those books." But when pressed as to what he really liked his face did light up and he even remembered the name of the book. "There was one book I've been reading," he burst out; "it's a fine book. It's called 'The Czar's Spy.'"

"Perhaps," suggested Ruth Hale of the visiting party, "a grand duke would say there was a lot of hokum in that."

Dempsey was not to be deterred by any such higher criticism. Never having been a grand duke, he did not worry about the accuracy of the story. It was in a field far apart from life. That we gathered was his idea of the proper field for fiction. In life Dempsey is a stern realist. It is only in reading that he is romantic. A more impressionable man would have been disturbed by the air of secrecy which surrounded the camp of Carpentier. That never worried Dempsey. He prepared himself and never thought

61

up contingencies. He did not even like to talk fight. None of us drew him out much about boxing. Somebody told him that Jim Corbett had reported that when he first met Carpentier he had been vastly tempted to make a feint at the Frenchman to see whether or not he would fall into a proper attitude of defense.

"Yes," giggled Dempsey, "and it would have been funny if Carp had busted him one on the chin." This seemed to him an extraordinary humorous conceit and he kept chuckling over it every now and then. While he was in this good humor somebody sounded him out as to what he would do if he lost; or rather the comment was made that an old time fighter, once a champion, was now coming back to the ring and had declared that he was as good as he ever was.

"Why shouldn't he?" said Dempsey just a little sharply. "Nobody wants to see a man that says he isn't as good as he used to be."

"Would you say that?" he was asked.

"Well," said Dempsey, and this time he reflected a little, "it would all depend on how I was fixed. If I needed the money I would. I'd use all the old alibis."

We liked that frankness and we liked Dempsey again when somebody wanted to know how he could possibly say anything in the ring during the fight to "get the goat of Carpentier." "We ain't nearly well enough acquainted for that," said Dempsey and we gathered that he was of the opinion that you must know a man pretty well before you can insult him. The champion is not a man to whom one would look for telling rejoinders, though he has needed them often enough in the last year and a half. Criticism has hurt him, for he is not insensitive. He is merely inarticulate. This must have been the reason which prompted some sporting writers to feel that he would come into the ring whipped and down from the fact that he had been able to make no reply to all the charges brought against him. It did not work out that way. Dempsey did have a means of expression and he used it. There is no logic in force and yet a man can exclaim "Is that so!" with his fists. Dempsey said it. If we may be allowed to stretch a point it might even be hazarded that the champion's motto is "Say it with cauliflowers."

As the Freudians have it, fighting is his "escape." Decidedly, he is a man with an inferiority complex. But for his boxing skill he would need literature badly. As it is, he does not need to read about hairbreadth escapes. He has them, such as in the second round of the fight on Boyle's Thirty Acres.

In summing up, we can only add that as yet literature has had no large effect upon the life of Jack Dempsey.

XI

For years we had been hearing about moral victories and at last we saw one. This is not intended
as an excuse for the fact that we said before the fight
that Carpentier would beat Dempsey. We erred
with Bernard Shaw. The surprising revelation which
came to us on this July afternoon was that a thing
may be done well enough to make victory entirely secondary. We have all heard, of course, of sport for
sport's sake but Georges Carpentier established a still
more glamorous ideal. Sport for art's sake was what
he . showed us in the big wooden saucer over on
Boyle's dirty acres.

It was the finest tragic performance in the lives of
ninety thousand persons. We hope that Professor
George Pierce Baker sent his class in dramatic com-
position. We will be disappointed if Eugene O'Neill,
the white hope of the American drama, was not there.
Here for once was a laboratory demonstration of life.
None of the crowds in Greece who went to somewhat
more beautiful stadiums in search of Euripides ever
saw the spirit of tragedy more truly presented. And
we will wager that Euripides was not able to lift his
crowd up upon its hind legs into a concerted shout of
"Medea! Medea! Medea!" as Carpentier moved

64

the fight fans over in Jersey City in the second round. In fact it is our contention that the fight between Dempsey and Carpentier was the most inspiring spectacle which America has seen in a generation.

Personally we would go further back than that. We would not accept a ticket for David and Goliath as a substitute. We remember that in that instance the little man won, but it was a spectacle less fine in artistry from the fact that it was less true to life. The tradition that Jack goes up the beanstalk and kills his giant, and that Little Red Ridinghood has the better of the wolf, and many other stories are limited in their inspirational quality by the fact that they are not true. They are stories that man has invented to console himself on winter's evenings for the fact that he is small and the universe is large. Carpentier showed us something far more thrilling. All of us who watched him know now that man cannot beat down fate, no matter how much his will may flame, but he can rock it back upon its heels when he puts all his heart and his shoulders into a blow.

That is what happened in the second round. Carpentier landed his straight right upon Dempsey's jaw and the champion, who was edging in toward him, shot back and then swayed forward. Dempsey's hands dropped to his side. He was an open target. Carpentier swung a terrific right hand uppercut and missed. Dempsey fell into a clinch and held on until his head cleared. He kept close to Carpentier during the rest of the fight and wore him down with body blows during the infighting. We know of course that when the first prehistoric creature crawled out of the

65

ooze up to the beaches (see "The Outline of History" by H. G. Wells, some place in the first volume, just a couple of pages after that picture of the big lizard) it was already settled that Carpentier was going to miss that uppercut. And naturally it was inevitable that he should have the worst of it at infighting. Fate gets us all in the clinches, but Eugene O'Neill and all our young writers of tragedy make a great mistake if they think that the poignancy of the fate of man lies in the fact that he is weak, pitiful and helpless. The tragedy of life is not that man loses but that he almost wins. Or, if you are intent on pointing out that his downfall is inevitable, that at least he completes the gesture of being on the eve of victory.

For just eleven seconds on the afternoon of July 2 we felt that we were at the threshold of a miracle. There was such flash and power in the right hand thrust of Carpentier's that we believed Dempsey would go down, and that fate would go with him and all the plans laid out in the days of the oozy friends of Mr. Wells. No sooner were the men in the ring together than it seemed just as certain that Dempsey would win as that the sun would come up on the morning of July 3. By and by we were not so sure about the sun. It might be down, we thought, and also out. It was included in the scope of Carpentier's punch, we feared. No, we did not exactly fear it. We respect the regularity of the universe by which we live, but we do not love it. If the blow had been as devastating as we first believed, we should have counted the world well lost.

Great circumstances produce great actors. History

is largely concerned with arranging good entrances
for people; and later exits not always quite so good.
Carpentier played his part perfectly down to the last
side. People who saw him just as he came before
the crowd reported that he was pitifully nervous,
drawn, haggard. It was the traditional and becoming
nervousness of the actor just before a great performance. It was gone the instant Carpentier came in
sight of his ninety thousand. His head was back and
his eyes and his smile flamed as he crawled through
the ropes. And he gave some curious flick to his
bathrobe as he turned to meet the applause. Until
that very moment we had been for Dempsey, but
suddenly we found ourself up on our feet making
silly noises. We shouted "Carpentier! Carpentier!
Carpentier!" and forgot even to be ashamed of our
pronunciation. He held his hands up over his head
and turned until the whole arena, including the five-
dollar seats, had come within the scope of his smile.

Dempsey came in a minute later and we could not
cheer, although we liked him. It would have been
like cheering for Niagara Falls at the moment somebody was about to go over in a barrel. Actually
there is a difference of sixteen pounds between the
two men, which is large enough, but it seemed that
afternoon as if it might have been a hundred. And
we knew for the first time that a man may smile and
smile and be an underdog.

We resented at once the law of gravity, the Mal-
thusian theory and the fact that a straight line is the
shortest distance between two points. Everything
scientific, exact, and inevitable was distasteful. We

67

wanted the man with the curves to win. It seemed impossible throughout the first round. Carpentier was first out of his corner and landed the first blow, a light but stinging left to the face. Then Dempsey closed in and even the people who paid only thirty dollars for their seats could hear the thump, thump of his short hooks as they beat upon the narrow stomach of Carpentier. The challenger was only too evidently tired when the round ended.

Then came the second and, after a moment of fiddling about, he shot his right hand to the jaw. Carpentier did it again, a second time, and this was the blow perfected by a life time of training. The time was perfect, the aim was perfect, every ounce of strength was in it. It was the blow which had downed Bombardier Wells, and Joe Beckett. It rocked Dempsey to his heels, but it broke Carpentier's hand. His best was not enough. There was an earthquake in Philistia but then out came the signs "Business as usual!" and Dempsey began to pound Carpentier in the stomach.

The challenger faded quickly in the third round, and in the fourth the end came. We all suffered when he went down the first time, but he was up again, and the second time was much worse. It was in this knockdown that his head sagged suddenly, after he struck the floor, and fell back upon the canvas. He was conscious and his legs moved a little, but they would not obey him. A gorgeous human will had been beaten down to a point where it would no longer function.

If you choose, that can stand as the last moment in

68

a completed piece of art. We are sentimental enough to wish to add the tag that after a few minutes Carpentier came out to the center of the ring and shook hands with Dempsey and at that moment he smiled again the same smile which we had seen at the beginning of the fight when he stood with his hands above his head. Nor is it altogether sentimental. We feel that one of the elements of tragedy lies in the fact that Fate gets nothing but the victories and the championships. Gesture and glamour remain with Man. No infighting can take that away from him. Jack Dempsey won fairly and squarely. He is a great fighter, perhaps the most efficient the world has ever known, but everybody came away from the arena talking about Carpentier. He wasn't every efficient. The experts say he fought an ill considered fight and should not have forced it. In using such a plan, they say, he might have lasted the whole twelve rounds. That was not the idea. As somebody has said, "Better four rounds of——" but we can't remember the rest of the quotation.

Dempsey won and Carpentier got all the glory. Perhaps we will have to enlarge our conception of tragedy, for that too is tragic.

XII

JACK THE GIANT KILLER

All the giants and most of the dragons were happy and contented folk. Neither fear nor shame was in them. They faced life squarely and liked it. And so they left no literature.

The business of writing was left to the dwarfs, who felt impelled to distort real values in order to make their own pitiful existence endurable. In their stories the little people earned ease of mind for themselves by making up yarns in which they killed giants, dragons and all the best people of the community who were too big and strong for them. Naturally, the giants and dragons merely laughed at such times as these highly drawn accounts of imaginary happenings were called to their attention.

But they laughed not only too soon but too long. Giants and dragons have died and the stories remain. The world believes to-day that St. George slew the dragon, and that Jack killed all those giants. The little man has imposed himself upon the world. Strength and size have come to be reproaches. The world has been won by the weak.

Undoubtedly, it is too late to do anything about this now. But there is a little dim and distant dragon blood in our veins. It boils when we hear the fairy stories and we remember the true version of Jack the Giant Killer, as it has been handed down by word of mouth in our family for a great many centuries. We can produce no tangible proofs, and we are willing to admit that the tale may have grown a little distorted here and there in the telling through the ages. Even so it sounds much more plausible to us than the one which has crept into the story books.

Jack was a Celt, a liar and a meager man. He had great green eyes and much practice in being pathetic. He could sing tenor and often did. But it was not in this manner that he lived. By trade he was a newspaper man though he called himself a journalist. In his shop there was a printing press and every afternoon he issued a newspaper which he called *Jack's Journal*. Under this name there ran the caption, "If you see it in *Jack's Journal* you may be sure that it actually occurred." Jack had no talent for brevity and little taste for truth. All in all he was a pretty poor newspaper man. We forgot to say that in addition to this he was exceedingly lazy. But he was a good liar.

This was the only thing which saved him. Day after day he would come to the office without a single item of local interest, and upon such occasions he made a practice of sitting down and making up something. Generally, it was far more thrilling than any of the real news of the community which clustered around one great highroad known as Main Street.

The town lay in a valley cupped between towering hills. On the hills, and beyond, lived the giants and

the dragons, but there was little interchange between these fine people and the dwarfs of the village. Occasionally, a sliced drive from the giants'
golf course would fall into the fields of the little
people, who would ignorantly set down the great
round object as a meteor from heaven. The giants
were considerate as well as kindly and they made
the territory of the little people out of bounds. Otherwise, an erratic golfer might easily have uprooted the
first national bank, the Second Baptist Church, which
stood next door, and *Jack's Journal* with one sweep
of his niblick. If by any chance he failed to get out
in one, the total destruction of mankind would have
been imminent.

Once upon a time, a charitable dowager dragon
sought to bring about a closer relationship between
the peoples of the hills and the valley in spite of
their difference in size. Hearing of a poor neglected
family in the village, which was freezing to death
because of want of coal, she leaned down from her
mountain and breathed gently against the roof of the
thatched cottage. Her intentions were excellent but
the damage was $152,694, little of which was covered
by insurance. After that the dragons and the giants
decided to stop trying to do favors for the little
people.

Being short of news one afternoon, Jack thought
of the great gulf which existed between his reading
public and the big fellows on the hill and decided
that it would be safe to romance a little. Accordingly, he wrote a highly circumstantial story of the
manner in which he had gone to the hills and killed

JACK THE GIANT KILLER

a large giant with nothing more than his good broad sword. The story was not accepted as gospel by all the subscribers, but it was well told, and it argued an undreamed of power in the arm of man. People wanted to believe and accordingly they did. Encouraged, Jack began to kill dragons and giants with greater frequency in his newspaper. In fact, he called his last evening edition *The Five Star Giant Final* and never failed to feature a killing in it under great red block type.

The news of the Jack's doings came finally to the hill people and they were much amused, that is all but one giant called Fee Fi Fo Fum. The Fo Fums (pronounced Fohum) were one of the oldest families in the hills. Jack supposed that all the names he was using were fictitious, but by some mischance or other he happened one afternoon to use Fee Fi Fo Fum as the name of his current victim. The name was common enough and undoubtedly the thing was an accident, but Mr. Fo Fum did not see it in that light. To make it worse, Jack had gone on in his story with some stuff about captive princesses just for the sake of sex appeal. Not only was Mr. Fo Fum an ardent Methodist, but his wife was jealous. There was a row in the Fo Fum home (see encyclopedia for Great Earthquake of 1007) and Fee swore revenge upon Jack.

"Make him print a retraction," said Mrs. Fo Fum.

"Retraction, nothing," roared Fee, "I'm going to eat up the presses."

Over the hills he went with giant strides and arrived at the office of *Jack's Journal* just at press time.

73

Mr. Fo Fum was a little calmer by now, but still revengeful. He spoke to Jack in a whisper which shook the building, and told him that he purposed to step on him and bite his press in two.

"Wait until I have this last page made up," said Jack.

"Killing more giants, I presume?" said Fee with heavy satire.

"Bagged three this afternoon," said Jack. "Hero Slaughters Trio of Titans."

"My name is Fo Fum," said the giant. Jack did not recognize it because of the trick pronunciation and the visitor had to explain.

"I'm sorry," said Jack, "but if you've come for extra copies of the paper in which your name figures I can't give you any. The edition is exhausted."

Fo Fum spluttered and blew a bale of paper out of the window.

"Cut that out," said Jack severely. "All complaints must be made in writing. And while I'm about it you forgot to put your name down on one of those slips at the desk in the reception room. Don't forget to fill in that space about what business you want to discuss with the editor."

Fo Fum started to roar, but Jack's high and pathetic tenor cut through the great bass like a ship's siren in a storm.

"If you don't quit shaking this building I'll call Julius the office boy and have him throw you out."

"Take the air," added Jack severely, disregarding the fact that Fo Fum before entering the office had found it necessary to remove the roof. But now the giant was beginning to stoop a little. His face grew purple and he was swaying unsteadily on his feet.

"Hold on a minute," said Jack briskly, "don't go just yet. Stick around a second."

He turned to his secretary and dictated two letters of congratulation to distant emperors and another to a cardinal. "Tell the Pope," he said in conclusion, "that his conduct is admirable. Tell him I said so."

"Now, Mr. Fo Fum," said Jack turning back to the giant, "what I want from you is a picture. There is still plenty of light. I'll call up the staff photographer. The north meadow will give us room. Of course, you will have to be taken lying down because as far as the *Journal* goes you're dead. And just one thing more. Could you by any chance let me have one of your ears for our reception room?"

Fo Fum had been growing more and more purple, but now he toppled over with a crash, carrying part of the building with him. Almost two years before he had been warned by a doctor of apoplexy and sudden anger. Jack did not wait for the verdict of any medical examiner. He seized the speaking tube and shouted down to the composing room, "Jim, take out that old head. Make it read, 'Hero Finishes Four Ferocious Foemen.' And say, Jim, I want you to be ready to replate for a special extra with an eight column cut. I'll have the photographer here in a second. I killed that last giant right here in the office. Yes, and say, Jim, you'd better use that stock cut of me at the bottom of the page. A caption, let me see, put it in twenty-four point cheltenham bold and make it read 'Jack—the Giant Killer.'"

75

XIII

JUDGE KRINK

H. 3d, our three-year-old son, has created for himself out of thin air somebody whom he can respect. The name of this character is Judge Krink, but generally he is more casually referred to as "the Judge." He lives, so we are informed, at some remote place called Fourace Hill. H. 3d says Judge Krink is his best friend. He told us yesterday that he had written a letter to Judge Krink and had received one in reply.

"What did you say?" we asked.

"I said I was writing him a letter."

"What did he say?"

"Nothing."

This interchange of courtesies did not seem epoch-making even in the life of a child, but we learned later just how extraordinarily important and useful Judge Krink had become to H. 3d. Cross-examination revealed the fact that Judge Krink has dirty hands which he never allows to be washed. Under no compulsion does he go to bed. Apparently he sits all day long in a garden, more democratically administered than any city park, digging dirt and putting it in a pail.

JUDGE KRINK

Candy Judge Krink eats very freely and without let or hindrance. In fact there is nothing forbidden to H. 3d which Judge Krink does not do with great gusto. Rules and prohibitions melt before the iron will and determination of the Judge. We suppose that when the artificial restrictions of a grown-up world bear too heavily upon H. 3d he finds consolation in the thought that somewhere in the world Judge Krink is doing all these things. We cannot get at Judge Krink and put him to bed or take away his trumpet. The Judge makes monkeys of all of us who seek to administer harsh laws in an unduly restricted world. The sound of his shovel beating against his tin pail echoes revolution all over the world.

And vicariously the will of H. 3d triumphs with him, no matter how complete may be any mere corporeal defeat which he himself suffers. The more we hear about the Judge the more strongly do we feel drawn to him. We would like to have one of our own. Some day we hope to win sufficient favor with H. 3d to prevail upon him to introduce us to Judge Krink.

We are never to meet Judge Krink after all. He has passed back into the nowhere from whence he came. It was only to-day that we learned the news, although we had suspected that the Judge's popularity was waning. Some visitor undertook to cross-question H. 3d about his relations with Krink and it was plain to see that the child resented it, but we

were not prepared for the direction which his revenge took. When we asked about the Judge to-day
there was no response at first and it was only after a
long pause that H. 3d answered, "I don't have
Judge Krink any more. He's got table manners."

XIV

Once there were three kings in the East and they were wise men. They read the heavens and they saw a certain strange star by which they knew that in a distant land the King of the world was to be born. The star beckoned to them and they made preparations for a long journey.

From their palaces they gathered rich gifts, gold and frankincense and myrrh. Great sacks of precious stuffs were loaded upon the backs of the camels which were to bear them on their journey. Everything was in readiness, but one of the wise men seemed perplexed and would not come at once to join his two companions who were eager and impatient to be on their way in the direction indicated by the star.

They were old, these two kings, and the other wise man was young. When they asked him he could not tell why he waited. He knew that his treasuries had been ransacked for rich gifts for the King of Kings. It seemed that there was nothing more which he could give, and yet he was not content.

He made no answer to the old men who shouted to him that the time had come. The camels were impatient and swayed and snarled. The shadows

79

across the desert grew longer. And still the young king sat and thought deeply.

At length he smiled, and he ordered his servants to open the great treasure sack upon the back of the first of his camels. Then he went into a high chamber to which he had not been since he was a child. He rummaged about and presently came out and approached the caravan. In his hand he carried something which glinted in the sun.

The kings thought that he bore some new gift more rare and precious than any which they had been able to find in all their treasure rooms. They bent down to see, and even the camel drivers peered from the backs of the great beasts to find out what it was which gleamed in the sun. They were curious about this last gift for which all the caravan had waited.

And the young king took a toy from his hand and placed it upon the sand. It was a dog of tin, painted white and speckled with black spots. Great patches of paint had worn away and left the metal clear, and that was why the toy shone in the sun as if it had been silver.

The youngest of the wise men turned a key in the side of the little black and white dog and then he stepped aside so that the kings and the camel drivers could see. The dog leaped high in the air and turned a somersault. He turned another and another and then fell over upon his side and lay there with a set and painted grin upon his face.

A child, the son of a camel driver, laughed and clapped his hands, but the kings were stern. They rebuked the youngest of the wise men and he paid no attention but called to his chief servant to make the first of all the camels kneel. Then he picked up the toy of tin and, opening the treasure sack, placed his last gift with his own hands in the mouth of the sack so that it rested safely upon the soft bags of incense.

"What folly has seized you?" cried the eldest of the wise men. "Is this a gift to bear to the King of Kings in the far country?"

And the young man answered and said: "For the King of Kings there are gifts of great richness, gold and frankincense and myrrh.

"But this," he said, "is for the child in Bethlehem!"

XV

THE EXCELSIOR MOVEMENT

The fun of most of the criticism of George Jean
Nathan's lies in the fact that he has been an ir-
reconcilable in the theater. Rules and theories have
been disclaimed by him. Each play has been a problem to be considered separately without relation to
anything else except, of course, the current dramatic
activities in Vienna, Budapest and Moscow. Most of
his themes have been variations of the two important
aspects of all criticism, "I like" and "I don't like."
Masking his thrusts under a screen of indifference,
he has generally afforded stirring comment by the
sudden revelation of the fact that his enthusiasms and
his hates are lively and personal. Being among the
unclassified, the element of surprise has entered
largely into his expression of opinion.

But of late it is evident that Mr. Nathan has grown
a little lonely in functioning as a guerilla in the field
of dramatic reviewing. He is envious of the cults
and his scorn of Clayton Hamilton, George Pierce
Baker and William Archer seems to have been nothing more than what the Frudians call a defensive
mechanism. He too would ally himself with a school
—to be called the George Jean Nathan School of
Criticism.

82

THE EXCELSIOR MOVEMENT

His latest volume of collected essays, entitled "The Critic and the Drama," is designed as a prospectus for pupils. It undertakes to codify and describe in part the theater of to-day and to analyze and explain much more fully George Jean Nathan. He insists on our knowing how the trick is done. To us there is something disturbing in all this. We have always been among those who did not care to go behind the scenes at the playhouse for fear that we might be forced to learn how thunder is contrived and the manner of making lightning. Still more we have feared that somebody would impel us into a corner and point out the real David Belasco. We much prefer our own romantic impression gathered wholly from his curtain speeches at first nights.

It is painful, then, to have the new book insist upon our meeting the real Mr. Nathan. It was not our desire ever to know how his mind worked. We much preferred to believe that the charming little pieces in the *Smart Set* had no father and no mother except spontaneous combustion. To find this antic author burdened with theories is almost as disillusioning as to hear of Pegasus winning the 2.20 trot or one of the muses contracting to give a culture course at the Woman's Study Club of New Rochelle.

And the worst of it is that the theories of Mr. Nathan, when exposed in detail, seem to be much like those of other men. Even those who have never had the privilege of attending a performance of Micklefluden's "Arbeit" at Das Hochhaus in Prague early in the spring of 1905 have much the same philosophy of the critic and the playhouse as Mr.

Nathan. Thus we find him explaining that Shakespeare was "the greatest dramatist who ever lived, because he alone of all dramatists most accurately sensed the mongrel nature of his art." Mr. Nathan also insists sternly that criticism must be personal, and in discussing the relation between the printed and the acted drama he ingeniously makes a comparison with music.

"If drama is not meant for actors," he cries, "may we not also argue that music is not meant for instruments?" We see no reason on earth why Mr. Nathan should not argue in this manner, since so many hundrds in the past have raised the same point. It is also interesting to learn that Mr. Nathan thinks that the drama can never approximate nature. "It holds the mirror not up to nature but to the spectator's individual nature." He has also discovered that "great drama, like great men and women, is always just a little sad."

"The Critic and the Drama" is probably the most profound book which Mr. Nathan has ever published and it is by far the dullest. His pages are alive with echoes even at such times as they are not directly evoked and called upon by name. One of the difficulties of profundity is overcrowding. A man may remain pretty much to himself as long as he chooses to keep his touch light and avoid research. Taking a suggestion from Mr. Nathan, it may be said that all great masses of men are a little serious. In the plains and the rolling country there is room for an individual to skip and frolic, but all the peaks are preempted.

84

THE EXCELSIOR MOVEMENT

It may not be generally known that the young man who carried the banner with the strange device was lucky to die when he did. Had he eventually reached the summit which he sought he would have discovered to his great dismay that he merely constituted the 29th division in the annual outing of the Excelsior Marching and Chowder Club.

Criticism gives the lie to an ancient adage. In this field of endeavor "The higher the fewer" may be recognized as an exquisite piece of irony.

XVI

THE DOG STAR

The Silent Call presents the most beautiful of all male stars now appearing in the films. In intelligence, also, his rank seems high. The picture is built around Strongheart, a magnificent police dog. There are, to be sure, minor two-legged persons in his support, but practically all the heavy emotional scenes are reserved for Strongheart.

The dog star has virtues which are all his own. Any man of such glorious physique could hardly fail to betray self-consciousness. His virility would obsess him to such an extent that there certainly would be moments of posturing and swagger. Strongheart is above all this. He never trades upon the fact of being a "he dog" or even emphasizes that he is red-blooded and 100 per cent police.

Unlike all the other handsome devils of the screen, he goes about his business without smirking. His smile is broad, unaffected and filled with teeth and tongue. And above all, Strongheart does not slick down his hair with water or with wax.

Fine mountain country has been selected for *The Silent Call* and we see Strongheart galloping like a racing snow plow through white meadows which foam at his progress. He fights villains with great

intensity and sincerity, devastates great herds of cattle and brings the picture to a fitting climax by leaping from a jutting cliff to drown a miscreant in a whirlpool. We have seen no photography as beautiful nor any picture so vivid and live in action.

The story itself is good enough, but somewhat less than masterly. Repetition dulls the edge of rescue. The heroine, for instance, never should have been allowed to visit God's own country without a chaperon. Her propensity for predicament seems unlimited. Let her be lost in a virgin forest, if only for a moment, and out of the nowhere some villain arises to buffet her with odious and violent attentions.

She keeps Strongheart as busy as if he had been a traffic police dog. He is forever engaged in indicating "Stop" and "Go" to the stream of miscreants who bear down upon Miss Betty Houston. Villainicular traffic in the Northwest woods seems to be in need of constant regulation.

Strongheart bit some bad men and barked at others. Both measures were effective, for this is an unusual dog in that his bark is just as bad as his bite. He never questioned the character or the intentions of the heroine. After all, he was only a dumb animal and his loyalty was tinged with no suspicions.

We must admit that the human frailty of doubt sometimes led us to carp a little at the rectitude of Miss Houston. Her plights were so numerous that we were mean enough to wonder whether all were accidental. There was one particular villain, for instance, who attempted to abduct her no less than four times. We could not dismiss the thought that

87

perhaps she had given him some encouragement. Indeed we would not have been surprised if at last there has come a caption quoting the heroine as saying: "Get along with you, dog, and mind your own business." This, however, did not prove to be within the scheme of the scenario writers.

In all justice to Miss Houston, it must be said that, though she owed Strongheart much, he was also in her debt. It took the love of a good woman to drag him back from degradation. He was a nice dog until his master left the ranch and went East to correct the proofs of a new book. Strongheart could not understand that and neither could we. It seemed to us as if the publisher might have sent the galleys on by mail.

Deprived of the care of his owner, Strongheart began to revert to type. He had been a wolf and he took to long hikes away from home. When he grew hungry he killed a cow. The cattle men put a price upon his head and Strongheart became an outcast.

His return to civilization was effected by the first attack upon Miss Houston. Even a wolf knows that it is only a coward who would strike a woman. The police instinct proved stronger than the call of the wild and the great beast bounded out of the thicket and seized Ash Brent by the trousers. This was the first of many meetings between Ash and Strongheart. The last and decisive encounter was in the whirlpool. The dog swam to the bank alone and sat upon the bank to howl the piercing death cry of the wolf.

There is a suggestion of a happy ending in *The Silent Call* because Strongheart's original master falls in love with Miss Houston and marries her. It was probably the only union for the heroine which the dog would have sanctioned, and yet we cannot imagine that it left him entirely happy. Once the much beset young woman was given over into the care of a good man, Strongheart must have realized that his vocation was gone. Ash Brent was dead and all the other villains had been captured by the Sheriff. Placidity stared Strongheart in the face.

To be sure, he bit people only because they were bad, but, like most reformers, he had learned to love his work. It was to him more than a duty. We doubt whether he remained long with the honeymooners. It is our notion that on the first dark night he took to the wilds again. We can imagine him stalking a contented cow in the moonlight. The poor beast lowers her head for grass and Strongheart, seeking to convince himself that the horns have been employed in an overt act, mutters: "You would, would you!" Then comes the leap and the crashing of the great wolf jaws. It is the invariable tragedy of the reformer that, though his work has been accomplished, he cannot retire. First come the giants and then the windmills.

XVII

ALTRUISTIC POKER

Although Ella Wheeler Wilcox's autobiography is a human document throughout, nothing in it has interested us quite so much as her description of her husband's poker system in the chapter called "The Compelling Lover."

"In my early married life," writes Mrs. Wilcox, "he was much in demand for the game of poker," but a little later she explains, "Even in his love of cards and in his monotonous life of travel for the first seven years after our marriage, when card games were his only recreation, he introduced his idea of altruism. This, too, was a matter known only to me. He played games of chance only with men he knew; whatever money he made was kept in a separate purse, and when he came home he asked me to help him distribute it among deserving people."

Any new system is worth trying when your luck is bad, and yet it seems to us that there are fundamental objections to the scheme suggested by Mrs. Wilcox. At least, we don't think it would work well for us. If we drew a club to four hearts we might bravely push all our chips forward and say "Raise it," provided the risk was ours alone. We couldn't do that if we were playing for Uncle Albert. Our anxiety would betray us. Even if Aunt Hattie had been mentally selected as the beneficiary of the evening we should feel compelled to play the cards close to our chest. She is a dear old lady and not a bit prudish, but we're sure she would never approve of whooping the pot on a king and an ace and a seven spot.

Then take the debatable question of two pairs. Personally we have always believed in raising on them before the draw. Such a procedure is dangerous, perhaps, but profitable in the long run. Under the Wilcox system it might be difficult to take the larger viewpoint. It is more than possible that we would grow timorous if Cousin Susie's hope of a comfortable old age rested upon eights and deuces.

Some years ago we used to encounter, every now and again, a kindly middle-aged gentleman who was playing to send his brother to Harvard. It weighed on him. Whenever he looked at his cards he had his brother's chance of an education in mind. In fact, he grew so excessively cautious that anybody could bluff him out of quite large pots merely by reaching for a white chip. Some of the players, we fear, used to take advantage of this fact. As we remember it, the young man finally went to the C. C. N. Y.

Of course, Ella Wheeler Wilcox makes no claim that the system is a winning one. The implication is quite the other way. After all, she writes of her husband, "He was much in demand for the game of poker."

91

XVIII

THE WELL MADE REVIEW

One of the simplest ways in which a critic can
put a play in its place is to refer to it as "well
made." The phrase has come to be a reproach. It
suggests a third act in which the friend of the family tells the husband, "Take her out and buy her a
good dinner," and the lover decides that he will go
back to Mesopotamia—— "Alone!"

George Bernard Shaw changed the style, and
taught playgoers to refuse to accept technic as something just as good as spiritual significance. We now
await the revolt against the well-made revue. Each
of the Ziegfeld Follies is perfect of its kind, but just
as in the plays of Pinero, form has triumphed over
substance. The name Ziegfeld on the label means a
magnificent product perfect in every detail with complete satisfaction guaranteed, but it is a standardized
product. You know just what you are going to get.
Ziegfeld scenery, Ziegfeld costumes mean something
definite. Even "a Ziegfeld chorus girl" suggests an
unvarying type. The hood is as unmistakable as
that of a Ford automobile.

At times one is struck with a longing to find a
single homely girl among all the merry marchers.
And there is at least a shadow of a wish to encounter,
likewise, something in a song or a set or a costume
rough, unfinished and ungainly. Alexander sighed

92

and so might Ziegfeld. His supremacy in the field of musical revue is unquestioned. Even the shows with which he has no connection follow his modes as best they can, though sometimes at a great distance. He really owes it to himself and to his public to put on, in the near future, a very bad revue so that in the ensuing year that most precious element in entertainment—surprise—may again come to the theater through him. The first of all the Ziegfeld Follies must have furnished its audience with a night of startled rapture. The rest have produced a pleasant evening.

Burdened by years of success, Mr. Ziegfeld must be hampered by innumerable rules about revue making. He has created tradition and probably it rises up in front of him now and again to bark his shins. The Follies is still an entertainment, but now it is also an institution. Plan, premeditation and the note of service must all have won their places in the making of each new show in the succession. The critic will not depart in peace until he has seen somehow, somewhere an altogether irresponsible revue. It will be produced not by Edward Royce but by spontaneous combustion. Some of it will be terrible. Few of the costumes will fit and many of them will be in bad taste. None of the tunes will be hummed by the audience as it leaves the theater. But, nevertheless and notwithstanding, this irresponsible revue of which I speak is going to contain two good jokes.

I had at least a glimmer of hope that *Shuffle Along* might be the first blow of the revolution against the well-made revue. Early explorers in the Sixty-Sec-

ona Street Music Hall came back glowing with dis-
covery. And yet after seeing the negro revue it seems
to me that stout Cortes and all his men were duped.
In book and music and dancing *Shuffle Along* follows Broadway tradition just as closely as it can. It
is rough with old things which have crumbled and
not with new things which are unfinished. And yet
it is easy to understand the thrill which swept through
some of the pioneers who were the first to see *Shuffle
Along*. In it there is one quality possessed by no
other show which has been seen in New York this
year. Most musical comedy performers seem to be
altruists who are putting themselves out to a great
extent in order to please you and the other paying
customers. *Shuffle Along* is entirely selfish. No
matter how enthusiastic the audience, it cannot possibly get as much fun out of the show as the performers. Not since the last trip to New York of the Triangle Club have I seen the amateur spirit more fully
realized in the theater. Perhaps the performers get
paid, but it does not seem fitting. The more engag-
ing theory is that each member of the chorus of
Shuffle Along who keeps his work up at top pitch until the end of the season receives a large blue sweater
with a white "S. A." on the front and is then allowed
to break training. The ten best performers, in addition, are tapped on the shoulder. There is a rumor
that social distinction as well as merit enters into this
selection, but it has never, to my knowledge, been con-
firmed.

Of course, nothing in the remarks above is to be
construed as implying that people in the Ziegfeld

choruses do not have a good time. Such a statement would certainly be far from the facts. As somebody or other has so aptly said, "It's great to be young and a Ziegfeld chorus girl." The difference is that no Caucasian chorister, including the Scandinavian, has the faculty of enjoying herself with the same frankness and abandon as the African. Centuries of civilization and weeks of training make it impossible. The Follies girl knows what she likes, but she has been taught not to point. A certain reserve and reticence is part of the Ziegfeld tradition. Even the most daring of Mr. Ziegfeld's experiments in summer costuming are more esthetic than erotic. Though the legs of the longest showgirl may be bare, one feels that she is clothed in reverence. When the lights begin to dim, and the soft music sounds to indicate that the current Ben Ali Haggin tableau is about to be disclosed, I am always a little nervous. So solemn and dignified is the entire atmosphere of the affair that I feel a little like a Peeping Tom in the presence of Godiva and generally I cover my eyes in order that they may be preserved for the final processional in which one girl will be Coal, another Aviation and a third the Monroe Doctrine.

The parade is one of the traditions of the Follies. "When in doubt make them march," is the way the rule reads in Mr. Ziegfeld's notebook. All of which opens the way to the suggestion that Mr. Ziegfeld should try the experiment some year of cutting about $100,000 out of his bill for costumes and using the money to buy a joke. In that case the marching chorus girls could pass a given point.

95

XIX

AN ADJECTIVE A DAY

It was a child in Hans Christian Andersen's fairy tale who finally told the truth by crying out, "He hasn't got anything on," as the king marched through the streets clad only in the magic cloth woven and cut by the swindling tailor. You may remember that everybody else kept silent because the tailor had given out that the cloth was visible only to such as were worthy of their position in life. The child knew nothing of this and anyway he didn't have any position in life, so he piped up and cried, "He hasn't got anything on." And though he was but a child others took up the cry, and finally even the king was convinced and ran to get his bathrobe. The tailor, as we remember the story, was executed.

In course of time that child grew up, and married, and died leaving heirs behind him. And they in turn were not so barren, so that to-day vast numbers of his descendants are in the world. Nearly all of them are critics of one sort or another, but mostly young critics. Like their great ancestor they are frank and shrill, and either valiant or foolhardy as you choose to look at it. Certainly they seldom hesitate to rush in. No, there is no doubt at all that they are just a wee bit hasty, these descendants of the child. It is rather useful that every now and then one of them should point a finger of scorn at some falsely great figure in the arts and cry out his nakedness at top voice. But sometimes they make mistakes. It has happened not infrequently that worthy and respectable artists and authors in great coats, close-fitting sack suits, and heavy woolen underwear, have been greeted by some member of the clan with the traditional cry, "He hasn't got anything on."

This may be embarrassing as well as unfair. Ever since the child scored his sensational critical success so many years ago, all his sons have been eager to do likewise. They have inherited extraordinary suspicion regarding the raiment of all great men. Even when they are forced to admit that some particular king is actually clad in substantial achievement of one sort or another, they are still apt to carp about the fit and cut of his clothing. Almost always they maintain that he borrowed his shoes from some one else and that he cannot fill them.

In regard to humbler citizens they are apt to carry charity to great lengths. In addition to the incident recorded by Andersen they cherish another legend about the child. According to the tradition, he wrote a will just before he died in which he said, "Thank heaven I leave not a single adjective to any of my descendants. I have spent them all."

The clan is notoriously extravagant. They live for all the world like Bedouins of the Sahara without thought of the possibility of a rainy day. Their gaudiest years come early in life. Middle age and beyond is apt to be tragic. Almost nothing in the experience of mankind is quite so heartrending as the spectacle of one of these young critics, grown gray, coming face to face in his declining years with a masterpiece. At such times he is apt to be seized with a tremor and stricken dumb. Undoubtedly he is tormented with the memory of all the adjectives which he flung away in his youth. They are gone beyond recall. He fumbles in his purse and finds nothing except small change worn smooth. The best he can do is to fling out a "highly creditable piece of work" and go on his way.

Still he has had fun for his adjectives for all that. There is a compensating glow in the heart of the young critic when he remembers the day an obscure author came to him asking bread, though rather expecting a stone, and he with a flourish reached down into the breadbox and gave the poor man layer cake.

"After all," one of the young critics told me in justifying his mode of life, "it may be just as tragic as you say to be caught late in life with a masterpiece in front of you and not a single adequate adjective left in your purse. Yes, I'll grant you that it's unfortunate. But there's still another contingency which I mean to avoid. Wouldn't it be a rotten sell to die with half your adjectives still unused? You know you can't take them with you to heaven. Of what possible use would they be up there? Even the bravest superlatives would seem pretty mean and petty in that land. Think of being blessed with milk and honey for the first time and trying to express your gratitude and wonder with, 'The best I ever tasted.' No, sir. I'm going to get ready for the new eternal words by using up all the old ones before I die."

XX

THE UNKNOWN SOLDIER

They call him "the unknown hero." It is enough, it is better that we should know him as "the unknown soldier." "Hero" suggests a superman and implies somebody exalted above his fellows. This man was one of many. We do not know what was in his heart when he died. It is entirely possible that he was a fearful man. He may even have gone unwillingly into the fight. That does not matter now. The important thing is that he was alive and is dead.

He was drawn from a far edge of the world by the war and in it he lost even his identity. War may have been well enough in the days when it was a game for heroes, but now it sweeps into the combat everything and every man within a nation. The unknown soldier stands for us as symbol of this blind and far-reaching fury of modern conflict. His death was in vain unless it helps us to see that the whole world is our business. No one is too great to be concerned with the affairs of mankind, and no one too humble.

The unknown soldier was a typical American and it is probable that once upon a time he used to speak of faraway folk as "those foreigners." He thought they were no kin of his, but he died in one of the distant lands. His blood and the blood of all the world mingled in a common stream.

The body of the unknown soldier has come home, but his spirit will wander with his brothers. There will be no rest for his soul until the great democracy of death has been translated into the unity of life.

XXI

A TORTOISE SHELL HOME

Every once in so often somebody gets up in a pulpit or on a platform and declares that home life in America is being destroyed. The agent of devastation varies. According to the mood of the man with forebodings, it is the motion pictures, the new dances, bridge, or the comic supplements in the Sunday newspapers. It seems to us that these defenders of the home are themselves offensively solicitous. If we happened to be a home, we rather think that we would resent the overeagerness of our champions. They act as if the thing they seek to preserve were so weak and pitiful that it must go down before the gust of any new enthusiasm.

After all, the home is much older than these dragons which are said to be capable of devouring it. Least of all are we disposed to worry over deadly effects from the new dances. This fear has recently been put into vivid form by Hartley Manners in a play called "The National Anthem," in which Laurette Taylor, his wife, was starred. Jazz, according to Mr. Manners, is our anthem. The hero and the heroine of his play dance themselves to the brink of perdition. The end is tragic, for the husband dies and the wife narrowly escapes from the effects of poison which she has taken by mistake while dazed from drink and dancing.

This seems to us special and exceptional. A vice must be easy to be universally dangerous. All the moralists assure us that descent by the primrose path is facile. Skill in the new dances argues to us a certain strength of character. We do not understand how any person of flabby will can become proficient. In our own case we must confess that it is not our strength and uprightness which has kept us from jazz, but such traits as timidity and lack of application. As a boy we painstakingly learned the two-step. For this we deserve no great credit. It was not our wish, and only the vigorous application of parental influence carried us through. After we broke away from the home ties we began to back-slide. The dances changed from month to month and we lacked the hardihood to keep up. Cravenly we quit and slumped into a job.

None of our excuses can be made persuasive enough for exoneration. All there is to be said for work as opposed to dancing is that it is so much easier. Of course, our respect is infinite for the sturdy ones who have gone through the flames of cleansing and perfecting fire and have earned the right to step out upon the waxed floor. Few of them escape the marks of their time of tribulation. Every close observer of American dancing must have noted the set expression upon the face of all participants. There is hardly one who might not serve as a model for General Grant exclaiming: "I propose to fight it out on this line if it takes all summer."

A TORTOISE SHELL HOME

No form of national activity begins to be so conscientious as dancing. Up-to-date physicians, we understand, are beginning to prescribe it as tonic and penance for patients growing slack in their attitude toward life. At a cabaret recently a man pointed out a dancer in the middle of the floor and said: "That woman in the bright red dress is fifty-six years old." We were properly surprised, and he went on: "Her story is interesting. Two years ago she went to a neurologist because of a general physical and nervous breakdown. He said to her: 'Madam, the trouble is that you are growing old, and, worse than that, you are ready to admit it. You must fight against it. You must hold on to youth as if it were a horizontal bar and chin yourself.'"

We looked at the woman more closely and saw that she was obeying the doctor's orders literally. Her fight was a gallant one. Dancing had served to keep down her weight and improve her blood pressure, but there was not the slightest suggestion that she was enjoying herself. She had bought advice and she was intent upon using it. And as we looked over the entire floor we could see no one who seemed to be dancing for the fun of it. A few took a pardonable pride in their perfection of fancy steps, but that emotion is not quite akin to joy. They were dancing for exercise or prestige, or to fulfill social obligations.

All this is admirable in its way, but we have not sufficient faith in the persistence of human gallantry to believe that it can last forever. The home will get every last one of the dancers yet because it is so much easier to loaf in an easy-chair than to keep up the continual bickering against old age, indolence, and the selfishness of comfort.

Motion pictures may be more dangerous because we are informed that they are still in their infancy. But perhaps the home is also. In spite of the length of time during which it has been going on, its possibilities of development are enormous. Within the memory of living man a home was generally supposed to be a place where people sat and stared at each other. Sometimes they visited neighbors, but these trips were traditionally restricted to occasions upon which the friends were ill and too helpless to carry on a conversation. If any one doubts that talk is a recent development in home life, let him consider the musical instruments of a generation which is gone. Take the spinnet, for instance, and note that even the most carefully modulated whisper would have drowned out its feeble tinkle.

To be sure, our ancestors had books and a few magazines, but they were not of a sort to promote general conversation. Only the grown-ups were capable of exchanging their views on Mr. Thackeray's latest novel. But now, when the group returns from an evening at the motion-picture theater where "The Kid" or "Shoulder Arms" is being shown, it is impossible to keep anybody out of the discussion on account of his lack of years. Little Ferdinand has just as much right to an opinion about the prowess of Charlie Chaplin as grandpa, and, according to our observation, it is a right almost certain to be exercised.

Of course, before we began this discussion of the

decay of home life we should have set about coming to some definition acceptable to both sides of the controversy. Now, when it is too late to do anything about it, we are struck by the fact that we are probably talking at cross purposes. It is our contention that man is not less than the turtle. We think it is entirely possible for him to carry his home life around with him. It would not seem to us, for instance, that home life was impaired if the family took in the movies now and again or even very frequently. Nor are we willing to accept a bridge party down the street as something alien and outside. In other words, a man's home (and, of course, we mean a woman's home as well) ought not to be defined by the walls of his house or even by the fences of the front yard. The anti-suffragists once had the slogan "Woman's place is in the home," but what they really meant was "in the house," since they used to insist that the business of voting would take her out of it. It seems to us that the woman of to-day should have a home with limits at least as spacious as those of the whole world. And so naturally she ought to have her share in all the concerns of life.

XXII

I'D DIE FOR DEAR OLD RUTGERS

"He fought the last twenty rounds with a broken hand." . "The final quarter was played on sheer nerve, for an examination at the end of the game showed that his backbone was shattered and both legs smashed." "Although knocked senseless in the opening chukker, he finished the match and no one realized his predicament until he confessed to his team mates in the clubhouse."

These are, of course, incidents common enough in the life of any of our sporting heroes. To a true American sportsman a set of tennis is held in about the same esteem as a popular playwright holds a woman's honor. There is no point at which "I give up" can be sanctioned. Not only must the amateur athlete sell his life dearly, but he must keep on selling it until he is carried off the field. Accordingly, it is easy to understand why Forest Hills seethed with indignation when Mlle. Suzanne Lenglen walked (she could still walk, mind you) over to an official in the middle of a tennis match and announced that she was ill and would not continue. It was quite obvious to all that the Frenchwoman was still alive and breathing and the thing was shocking heresy.

106

I'D DIE FOR OLD RUTGERS

The writer is not disposed to defend Suzanne's heresy to the full. He believes that Mlle. Lenglen was ill, but he feels that she erred, not because she resigned, but because she did it with so little grace. She seemed to have no appreciation of the hardship which the sudden termination of the match imposed upon Mrs. Molla Bjurstedt Mallory. However, Molla did and came off the court swearing.

It was an embarrassing moment, but possibly a moral can be dug from it all the same. For the first time in the experience of many, a new sort of athletic tradition was vividly presented. No one will deny that the French knew the gesture of Thermopylæ as well as the next one, but they have never thought to associate it with sports. The gorgeous and gallant Carpentier has, upon occasions in his ring career, resigned. He showed no lack of nerve on these occasions, but merely followed a line of conduct which is foreign to us. Pitted at those particular times against men who were too heavy for him and facing certain defeat, he admitted their superiority somewhat before the inevitable end. Like a chess master, he sensed the fact that victory was no longer in the balance, and that nothing remained to be done except some mopping up. Such perfunctory and merely academic action did not seem to him to come properly within the realm of sport, particularly if he was to be the man mopped up.

American sport commentators who knew these facts in the record of Carpentier were disposed to announce before his match with Dempsey that he would most certainly seek to avoid a knockout by

107

stopping as soon as he was hurt. His astounding courage surprised them. And yet it was exactly the sort of courage they should have expected. He did not fight on through gruelling punishment just for the sake of being a martyr. He went through it because up to the very end he believed that his great right hand punch might win for him, and even at the last Carpentier was still swinging.

In spite of the sentimental objections of the old-fashioned follower of sports, the tradition which was bred out of Sparta by Anglo-Saxon has begun to decay. Referees do step in and end unequal contests. Ring followers themselves are known to cry, "Stop the fight" at times when the match has become no longer a contest. "Mollycoddles!" shriek the ghosts of the bareknuckle days who float over the ring, but we do not heed their voices. Again, we have decreasing patience with the severely injured football player who struggles against the restraining arms of the coaches when they would take him out because of his disabilities. To-day he is less a hero than a rather dramatically self-conscious young man who puts a gesture above the success of his team.

There is still ground for the modification of a sporting tradition which has made those things which we call games become at moments ordeals having no relation to sport. Losing is still considered such a serious business that an elaborate ritual has been built up as to what constitutes good losing. We not only demand that a man shall die, if need be, for the Lawn Tennis Championship of Eastern Rhode Island, but we go so far as to prescribe the exact manner in which he shall die. A set, silent and determined demeanor is generally favored.

From Japan have come hints of something better in this direction. Every American engaged in sport should be required to spend an afternoon in watching Zenzo Shimidzu of the Japanese Davis Cup team. Shimidzu's contribution to sport is the revelation that a man may try hard and yet have lots of fun even when things go against him. He seems to reserve his most winning smile for his losing shots. Once in his match against Bill Johnston he was within a point of set and down from the sky a high short lob was descending. Shimidzu was ready for what seemed a certain kill. He was as eager as an avenging sparrow. Back came his racquet and down it swung upon the ball, only to drive it a foot out of court. Immediately, the little man burst into a silent gale of merriment. The fact that he had a set within his grasp and had thrown it away seemed to him almost the funniest thing which had ever happened to him.

Of course, this is a manner which might be difficult for us Americans to acquire. Unlike the Japanese we have only a limited sense of humor. Its limits end for the most part with things which happen to other people. We laugh at the pictures in which we see Happy Hooligan being kicked by the mule, but we would not be able to laugh if we ourselves met the same mule under similar circumstances. However, in an effort to popularize the light and easy demeanor in sporting competition it is fair to point out that it is not only a beautiful thing but that it is also effective.

109

Shimidzu almost beat Tilden by the very fact that he refused to do anything but smile when things went against him. The tall American would smash a ball to a far corner of the court for what seemed a certain kill, but the little man would leap across the turf and send it back. And as he stroked the ball he smiled. It was discouraging enough for Tilden to be pitted against a Gibraltar, but it seemed still more hopeless from the fact that even when he managed to split the rock it broke only into the broadest of grins.

Ten years of work by one of our most prominent editors for a war with Japan were swept away by the Davis Cup matches. It is hard to understand how there can be any race problem concerning a people with so excellent a backhand and so genial a disposition. Indeed, many of the things which our friends from California have told us about Japan did not seem to be so. All of us have heard endlessly about the rapidity with which the Japanese increase. There was no proof of it at Forest Hills. When the doubles match started there were on one side of the net two Japanese. When the match ended, almost four hours later, there was still just two Japanese.

XXIII

One of the characters in "A Prince There Was" is the editor of a magazine and, curiously enough, he has been made the hero of the film. Of course, there may be something to be said for editors. Indeed, we have heard them trying to say it, and yet they remain among the forces of darkness and of mystery. By every rule of logic the editor in any story ought to be the villain.

It is not the darkness so much as the mystery which disturbs us. Only rarely have we been able to understand what an editor was talking about. Sometimes we have suspected that neither of us did. There was, for instance, the man who tapped upon his flat-topped desk and said with great precision and deliberation, "When you are writing for *Blank's Magazine*, you want to remember that *Blank's* is a magazine which is read at five o'clock in the afternoon."

He was our first editor. Disillusion had not yet set in. We still believed in Santa Claus and sanctums. And so we took home with us the advice about five o'clock and pondered. We remembered it perfectly, but that was not much good. "*Blank's* is a magazine which is read at five o'clock in the after-

111

noon." How were we to interpret this declaration of a principle? It was beyond our powers to write with ladyfingers. Possibly the editor meant that our style needed a little more lemon in it. There could be no complaint, we felt sure, against the sugar. Ten years of hard service on a New York morning newspaper had granulated us pretty thoroughly.

Having made up our mind that a slight increase in the acid content per column might enable us to qualify with the editor as a man who could write for five o'clock in the afternoon, we were suddenly confronted with a new problem. *Blank's* was an international magazine. Did the editor mean five o'clock by London or San Francisco time? Until we knew the answer there was no good running our head against rejection slips. There was no way to tell whether he would like an essay entitled "On Pipe Smoking Before Breakfast in Surrey," or whether he would prefer a little something on "Is the Garden of Eden Mentioned in the Bible Actually California?" Naturally, if one were writing with San Francisco's five o'clock in mind he would go on to make some comparison between Los Angeles and the serpent.

After extended deliberation, we decided that perhaps it would be best not to try to write for *Blank's* at all. It might put a strain upon the versatility of a young man too hard for him to bear. Suppose, for instance, he worked faithfully and molded his style to meet all the demands and requirements of five o'clock in the afternoon, and then suppose just as he was in the middle of a long novel, daylight saving should be introduced? His art would then be exactly one hour off and he would be obliged to turn back his hands along with those of the clock.

Of course, even though you understand an editor you may not agree with him. The makers of magazines incline a little to dogma. Give a man a swivel chair and he will begin to lean back and tell you what the public wants. Gazing through his window over the throng of Broadway, a faraway look will come into his eyes and he will begin to speak very earnestly about the farmer in Iowa. The farmer in Iowa is enormously convenient to editors. He is as handy as a rejection slip. In refusing manuscripts which he doesn't want to take, an editor almost invariably blames it on some distant subscriber. "I like this very much myself," he will explain. "It's great stuff. I wish I could use it. That part about the bobbed hair is a scream. But none of it would mean anything to the farmer in Iowa. Won't you show me something again that isn't quite so sophisticated?"

Riding through Iowa, we always make it a point to shake our fist at the landscape. And if by any chance the train passes a farmer we try to hit him with some handy missile. And why not? He kept us out of print. At least they said he did.

And yet though editors are invariably doleful about the capacity of the farmer in Iowa and points west, it would be quite inaccurate to suggest any fundamental pessimism. An editor is always optimistic, particularly when a contributor asks for his check. But it really is a sincere and deep grained hopefulness. No editor could live from day to day

without the faculty or arguing himself into the belief
that the next number of his magazine is not going to
be quite so bad as the last one.

Unfortunately he is not content to be a solitary
tippler in good cheer. He feels that it is his duty to
discover authors and inspirit them. Indeed, the
average editor cannot escape feeling that telling a
writer to do something is almost the same thing as
performing it himself.

The editorial mind, so called, is afflicted with the
King Cole complex. Types subject to this delusion
are apt to believe that all they need do to get a thing
is to call for it. You may remember that King Cole
called for his bowl just as if there were no such thing
as a Volstead amendment. "What we want is humor,"
says an editor, and he expects the unfortunate author
to trot around the corner and come back with a quart
of quips.

An editor would classify "What we want is humor"
as a piece of coöperation on his part. It seems to
him a perfect division of labor. After all, nothing
remains for the author to do except to write.

Sometimes the mogul of a magazine will be even
more specific. We confessed to an editor once that
we were not very fertile in ideas, and he said, "Never
mind, I'll think up something for you."

"Let me see," he continued, and crinkled his brow
in that profound way which editors have. Suddenly
the wrinkles vanished and his face lighted up.
"That's it," he cried. "I want you to go and do us a
series something like Mr. Dooley." He leaned back
and fairly beamed satisfaction. He had done his

best to make a humorist out of us. If failure followed it could only be because of shortsightedness and stubbornness on our part. We had our assignment.

XXIV

WE HAVE WITH US THIS EVENING——

We have always wondered just what it is which frightens the after dinner speaker. He is protected by tradition, the Christian religion and the game laws. And yet he trembles. Perhaps he knows that he is going to be terrible, but it is common knowledge that after dinner speakers seldom reform. The life gets them. It was thought, once upon a time, that the practice was in some way connected with alcoholic stimulation, but this has since been disproved. After dinner speaking is a separate vice. Total abstainers from every other evil practice are not immune.

The chief fault is that an irrationally inverted formula has come into being. The after dinner speaker almost invariably begins with his apology. He is generally becomingly frank when he first gets to his feet. There is always a confident prophecy that the audience is not going to be very much interested in what he has to say and the admission that he is pretty sure to do the job badly. Unfortunately, no speaker ever succeeds in deterring himself by these forebodings of disaster. He never fails to go on and prove the truth of his own estimate of inefficiency.

Many men profess to find the greatest difficulty in getting to their feet. Perhaps this is sincere, but the

116

task does not seem to be one-sixteenth as hard as sitting down again. People whose vision is perfect in every other respect suffer from a curious astigmatism which prevents them from recognizing a stopping point when they come to it. We suggest to some ingenious inventor that he devise a combination of time clock and trip hammer by which a dull, blunt instrument shall be liberated at the end of five minutes so that it may fall with great force, killing the after dinner speaker and amusing the spectators. The mechanical difficulties might be great, but the machine would be even more useful if it could be attuned in some way so that the hammer should fall, if necessary, before the expiration of the five minutes, the instant the speaker said, "That reminds me of the story about the two Irishmen."

Funny stories are endurable, in moderation, if only the teller is perfectly frank in introducing them for their own sake and not pretending that they have any conceivable relationship to the endowment fund of Wellesley College, or the present condition of the silk business in America. To such length has hypocrisy gone, that there is now at large and dining out, a gentleman who makes a practice of kicking the leg of the table and then remarking, "Doesn't that sound like a cannon?—Speaking of cannon, that reminds me——"

Another young man of our own acquaintance has been using the same anecdote for all sorts of occasions for the last four years. His story concerns an American soldier who drove a four-mule team past the first line trench in the darkness and started rum-

bling along an old road that led across no-man's-
land. He had gone a few yards when a doughboy
jumped up out of a listening post and began to signal
to him. "What's the matter?" shouted the driver.

"Shush! Shush!" hissed the outpost with great
terror and intensity. "You're driving right toward
the German lines. For Heaven's sake go back and
don't speak above a whisper."

"Whisper, Hell!" roared the driver. "I've got to
turn four mules around."

It may be that there actually was such an outpost
and such a driver, but neither had any intention of
acting as a perpetual symbol and yet we know positively that this particular story has been introduced
as an argument for buying another Liberty Bond of
the fourth issue; as a justification for the vehemence
of the American novelists of the younger generation;
and as a reason for the tendency to overstatement in
the dramatic and literary criticism of New York
newspapers. We are also under the impression that
it was used in a debate concerning the propriety of a
motion picture censorship in New York state.

Indeed the speaker whom we have in mind never
failed to use the mule story, no matter what the
nature of the occasion, unless he substituted the one
about the man who wanted to go to Seville. He was
a farmer, this man, and he lived some few miles
away from Seville in a little ramshackle farm house.
It had been his ambition of a lifetime to go to Seville
and upon one particular morning he came out of the
house carrying a suitcase.

"Where are you going?" asked his wife.

"To Seville," replied the farmer.

His wife was a very pious woman and she added by way of correction, "You mean, God willing."

"No," objected the farmer, dogmatically, "I mean I'm going to Seville."

Now Heaven was angered by this impiety and the dogmatic farmer was immediately transformed into a frog. Before the very eyes of his wife he lost his mortal form and hopped with a great splash into the big pond behind the house. To that pond the good woman went every day for a year and prayed that her husband should be restored to his natural form. On the first morning of the second year the big frog began to grow bigger and bigger and suddenly he was no longer a frog but a man. Out of the pond he leaped and ran straightaway into the house. He came out carrying a suitcase.

"Where are you going?" exclaimed the startled wife.

"To Seville," said the farmer.

"You mean," his wife implored in abject terror, "God willing."

"No," answered the farmer, "to Seville or back to the frog pond!"

The young man of whom we are writing first heard the story from Major General Robert Lee Bullard in a training school in Lyons. The doughty warrior told it in reply to the question, "What is this offensive spirit of which you've been telling us?" But with a sea change the story took up many other and varied rôles. It served as the climax of an eloquent speech in favor of the release of political prisoners; it began

119

an address urging greater originality upon the dramatists of America and it was conscripted at a luncheon to Hughie Jennings to explain the speaker's interpretation of the fundamental reason for the victory of the New York Giants over the Yankees in the world's series of last season.

Speaking of baseball, a great football coach once said that he could develop a championship eleven any time at all out of good material and seven simple plays well learned. Likewise, an after-dinner speaker can manage tolerably well with a limited supply of stories, if only they are elastic enough in interpretation and he covers a sufficiently wide range of territory in his dining rambles.

It is our experience that the most inveterate story tellers among public speakers are ministers. Unfortunately, the average clergyman has a tendency to select tales a little rowdy in an effort to set himself down among his listeners as a fellow member in good standing of the fraternity of Adam. Still more unfortunately the ministerial speaker often attempts to modify and deodorize the anecdote a little and, on top of that, gets it just a little wrong. No matter who the narrator may be, nothing is quite so ghastly as the improper story when told to an audience of more than ten or eleven listeners. Even more than a poetic drama a purple story needs a group, small and select. Any one interested in preserving impropriety might very well endow a chain of thimble theaters with a maximum seating capacity of ten. Some such step is needed or the off color yarn will disappear entirely from American life. It was nurtured upon big mirrors and brass rails and, these being lacking, there is no proper atmosphere in which it may suitably be reared. Most certainly the anecdote of doubtful character does not belong to large banquets even of visiting Elks. Literature of this sort is fragile. It represents what the Freudians call an escape, and the most brazen of us is a little shamefaced about taking off his inhibitions in front of a hundred people, mostly strangers.

There must be something wrong with after-dinner speaking because it is notoriously the lowest form of American oratory. It if were not for Chauncey M. Depew whole generations in this country would have been born and lived and died without once having any memory worth preserving after the demitasse. The trouble, we think, is that dinner guests are much too friendly. It is the custom that the man at the speakers' table may not be heckled. He is privileged and privilege has made him dull. According to our observation there is never anything of interest said with the laying of cornerstones or the dedication of new high school buildings. On the other hand, we have frequently been amused and excited by tilts at political conventions and mass meetings.

William Jennings Bryan is among the prize bores of the world when he gets up to do his canned material about *The Prince of Peace*, but no sensitive soul can fail to admire this same Commoner if he has ever .had the privilege of hearing him talk down political foes upon the floor of a convention. All the labored tricks of oratory are forgotten then. Give Mr. Bryan some one at whom he may with propriety

121

shake a finger and he becomes direct, vivid and moving.

Colonel Theodore Roosevelt was a speaker of somewhat the same type. He did not talk well unless there was some living and present person for him to speak against. Upon one occasion we heard him make a particularly dreary discourse, and incidentally a political one, until he came to a point where a group in the audience took exception to some statement and attempted to howl him down. It was like the touch of a whip on the flanks of a stake horse. Roosevelt returned to the statement and said it over again, only this time he said it much more dogmatically and twice as well. Before that speech was done he had climbed to the top of a table and was putting all his back and shoulders into every word. Even his platitudes seemed to be knockout blows. He was inspiring. He was magnificent.

The after-dinner speaker needs this same stimulus of emotion. He ought to have something into which he can get his teeth. Every well conducted banquet should include a special committee to heckle the guests of honor. Even a dreary person might be aroused to fervor if his opening sentence was met with a mocking roar of, "Is that so!" Loud cries of "Make him sit down" would undoubtedly serve to make the speaker forget his entire stock of anecdotes about Pat and Mike. There would be no calm in which he could be reminded of anything except that certain desperadoes were not willing to listen, and that, by the Old Harry, he was going to give it to them so hot and heavy that they would have to.

The scheme may sound a little cruel, but we ought to face the fact that a time has come when we must choose between cutting off the heads of our after-dinner speakers or slapping them in the face. We believe that they deserve to have a chance to show us whether or not they have a right to live.

XXV

THE YOUNG PESSIMISTS

Bert Williams used to tell a story about a man on a lonely road at night who suddenly saw a ghost come out of the forest and begin to follow him. The man walked faster and the ghost increased his pace. Then the man broke into a run with the ghost right on his heels. Mile after mile, faster and faster, they went until at last the man dropped at the side of the road exhausted. The ghost perched beside him on a large rock and boomed, "That was quite a run we had." "Yes" gasped the man, "and as soon as I get my breath we're going to have another one."

Our young American pessimists see man at the moment he drops beside the road, and without further investigation decide that it is all up with him. To be sure, they may not be very far wrong in the ultimate fate of man, but at least they anticipate his end. They do not stick with him until the finish; and this second-wind flight, however useless, is something so characteristic of life that it belongs in the record. I have at least a sneaking suspicion that now and again there happens along a runner so staunch and courageous that he keeps up the fight until cock-crow and thus escapes all the apparitions which would overthrow him. Of course, it is a long shot and the young pessimists are much too logical to wait for such miraculous chances. As a matter of fact, they don't call themselves pessimists, but prefer to be known as rationalists, realists, or some such name which carries with it the hint of wisdom.

And they are wise up to the very point of believing only the things they have seen. However, I am not sure they are quite so wise when they go a notch beyond this and assert roundly that everything which they have seen is true. For my own part I don't believe that white rabbits are actually born in high hats. The truth is quicker than the eye, but it is hardly possible to make any person with fresh young sight believe that. Question the validity of some character in a play or book by a young rationalist and he will invariably reply, "Why she lived right in our town," and he will upon request supply name, address, and telephone number to confound the doubters.

"Let the captious be sure they know their Emmas as well as I do before they tell me how she would act," wrote Eugene O'Neill when somebody objected that the heroine of "Diff'rent" was not true. This, of course, shifts the scope of the inquiry to the question, "How well does O'Neill know his Emmas?" Indeed, how well does any bitter-end rationalist know anybody? Once upon a time we lived in a simple age in which when a man said, "I'm going to kick you downstairs because I don't like you," and then did it, there was not a shadow of doubt in the mind of the person at the foot of the stairs that he had come upon an enemy. All that is changed now. During the war, for instance, George Sylvester Viereck wrote a book to prove that every time Roosevelt said, "Viereck is an undesirable citizen," or words to that effect, he was simply dissembling an admiration so great that it was shot through and through with ambivalent outbursts of hatred. Mr. Viereck may not have proved his case, but he did, at least, put his relations into debatable ground by shifting from Philip conscious to Philip subconscious.

In the new world of the psychoanalysts there is confusion for the rationalist even though he is dealing with something so inferentially logical as a science. For here, with all its tangible symbols, is a science which deals with things which cannot be seen or heard or touched. And much of all the truth in the world lies in just such dim dominions. The pessimist is very apt to be stopped at the border. For years he has reproached the optimist with the charge that he lived by dreams rather than realities. Now, wise men have come forward to say that the key to all the most important things in life lies in dreams. Of course, the poets have known that for years, but nobody paid any attention to them because they only felt it and offered no papers to the medical journals.

It would be unfair to suggest that no dreamer is a pessimist. The most prolific period of pessimism comes at twenty-one, or thereabouts, when the first attempt is made to translate dreams into reality, an attempt by a person not over-skillful in either language. Often it is made in college where a new freedom inspires a somewhat sudden and wholesale attempt to put every vision to the test. Along about this time the young man finds that the romanticists have lied to him about love and he bounces all the way back to Strindberg. Maybe he gets drunk for the first time and learns that every English author from Shakespeare to Dickens has vastly overrrated it for literary effect. He follows the formulæ of Falstaff and instead of achieving a roaring joviality he goes to sleep. Personally tobacco sent me into a deep pessimism when I first took it up in a serious way. Huck's corncob pipe had always seemed to me one of the most persuasive symbols of true enjoyment. It seemed to me that life could hold nothing more ideal than to float down the Mississippi blowing rings. After six months of experimenting I was ready to believe that maybe the Mississippi wasn't so much either. Romance seemed pretty doubtful stuff. Around this time, also, the young man generally discovers, in compulsory chapel, that the average minister is a dull preacher; and of course that knocks all the theories of the immortality of the soul right on the head. He may even have come to college with a thirst for knowledge and a faith in its exciting quality, only to have these emotions ooze away during the second month of introductory lectures on anthropology.

Accordingly, it is not surprising to find F. Scott Fitzgerald's Amory Blaine looking at the towers of Princeton and musing:

Here was a new generation, shouting the old cries, learning the old creeds through a revery of long days and

127

nights; destined finally to go out into that dirty gray turmoil to follow love and pride; a new generation dedicated
more than the last to the fear of poverty and the worship
of success; grown up to find all Gods dead, all wars fought;
all faiths in man shaken. . . .

Nobody wrote as well as that in Copeland's course
at Harvard but there was a pretty general agreement
that life—or rather Life—was a sham and a delusion. This was expressed in poems lamenting the
fact that the oceans and the mountains were going to
go on and that the writer wouldn't.
Generally he didn't give the oceans or the mountains very long either. All the short stories were
about murder and madness. We cut our patterns
into very definite conclusions because we were pessimists and sure of ourselves. It was the most logical
of philosophies and disposed of all loose ends. One
of my pieces (to polish off a theme on the futility of
human wishes) was about a man who went stark
raving, and Copeland sat in his chair and groaned
and moaned, which was his substitute for making
little marks in red ink. He had been reading Sheri-
dan's "The Critic" to the class with the scene in which
the two faithless Spanish lovers and the two nieces
and the two uncles all try to kill each other at the
same time, and are thus thrown into the most terrific
stalemate until the author's ingenious contrivance of
a beefeater who cries, "Drop your weapons in the
Queen's name." At any rate when I had finished the
little man ceased groaning and shook his head about
my story of the man who went mad. "Broun," he
said, "try to solve your problems without recourse to

death, madness—or any other beefeater in the Queen's name."

And it seems to me that the young pessimists, generally speaking, have allowed themselves to be bound in a formula as tight as that which ever afflicted any Pollyanna. It isn't the somberness with which they imbue life which arouses our protest, so much as the regularity. They paint life not only as a fake fight in which only one result is possible, but they make it again and again the selfsame fight.

XXVI

GLASS SLIPPERS BY THE GROSS

When Cinderella sat in the ashes she should have consoled herself with the thought of the motion-picture rights. No young woman of our time has had her adventures so ceaselessly celebrated in film and drama. Of course, she generally goes by some other name. It might be "Miss Lulu Bett," for instance.

For our part, we must confess that much as we like Zona Gale's modern and middle-western version of the old tale, Cinderella is beginning to lose favor with us. Her appeal in the first place rested on the fact that she was abused and neglected, but by this time the ashes have become the skimpiest sort of interlude. You just know that the fairy godmother is waiting in the wings, and you can hear the great coach honking around the corner. Undoubtedly, the order for the glass slippers was placed months in advance. More than likely it called for a gross, since there are ever so many Cinderella feet to, fit these days—what with Peg and Kiki and Sally and Irene and all the authentic members of the family. Indeed, for a time, Cinderella was spreading herself around so lavishly in dramatic fiction that one sex was not enough to contain her, and we had a Cinderella Man. All the usual perquisites were his except the glass slipper.

And now the time has come when the original poetic justice due to the miss by the kitchen stove has quite worn off. Cinderella has been paid in full, but how about her two ugly sisters? They have gone down the ages without honor or rewards. Each time their aspirations are blighted. Although eminently conscientious in fulfilling their social duties, it has availed them nothing. We are determined not to welcome the story again until it appears in a revised form. In the version which we favor, Prince Charming will try the glass slipper upon Cinderella, and then turn away without enthusiasm, remarking in cutting manner, "It is not a fit. Your foot is much too small." One of the ugly sisters will be sitting somewhat timidly in the background, and it will be to her the Prince will turn, exclaiming rapturously: "A perfect number nine!"

And they lived happily ever after.

And while we are about it, a good many of the fairy stories can stand revision. This Jack the Giant Killer has been permitted to go to outrageous lengths. Between him and David, and a few others, the impression has been spread broadcast that any large person is a perfect setup for the first valiant little man who chooses to assail him with sword or sling. We purpose organizing the Six Foot League to combat this hostile propaganda. Elephants will be admitted, too, on account of the unjust canard concerning their fear of mice. We and the elephants do not intend to go on through life taking all sorts of nonsense

131

from whippersnappers. The success of Jack and all
the other little men of legend has undoubtedly been
due to the chivalry of the big and strong. Dragons
have died cheerfully rather than take a mean advantage and slay pestiferous and belligerent runts by
spitting out a little fire. Why doesn't somebody
celebrate the heroism of these miscalled monsters
who have gone down with full steam in their boilers
because they were unwilling even to guard themselves
against foemen so palpably out of their class?

Take St. George, for instance. Do you imagine
for a minute that his victory was honestly and fairly
earned? British pluck and all the rest of it had
nothing to do with it. The dragon could have finished
him off in a second, but the huge and kindly animal
was afflicted with an acute sense of humor. Between
paroxysms it is known to have remarked: "I shall
certainly die laughing." It could not resist the sight
of St. George swaggering up to the attack in full
armor like an infuriated Ford charging the Wool-
worth Building. And the strangest part of it all is
that the dragon did die laughing just as it had predicted. St. George flung his sword exactly between
a "ha" and a "ha." The tiny bit of steel lodged in
the windpipe like a fishbone, and before medical
assistance could be summoned the dragon was dead.
Of course it was clever, but we should hardly call it
cricket. All the triumphs of the little men are of
much the same sort. Honest, slam-bang, line play
has never entered into their scheme of things. Their
reputation rests on fakes and forward passes.

Then there was the wolf and Little Red Riding-

Hood. The general impression seems to be that the child's grandmother was a saintly old lady and that the wolf was a beast. Let us dismiss this sentimental conception and consider the facts squarely. Before meeting the wolf Red Riding-Hood was the usual empty-headed flapper. She knew nothing of the world. So flagrant was her innocence that it constituted a positive menace to the community. The wolf changed all that. It gave Red Riding-Hood a good scare and opened her eyes. After that encounter nobody ever fooled Red Riding-Hood much. She positively abandoned her practice of wandering around into cottages on the assumption that if there was anybody in bed it must be her grandmother.

The familiar story, somehow or other, has omitted to say that Miss Hood eventually married the richest man in the village. Perhaps the old narrator did not want to reveal the fact that on top of the what-not in the palatial home there stood a silver frame, and upon the picture in the frame was written: "Whatever measure of success I may have attained I owe to you—Red Riding-Hood." And whose picture do you suppose it was? Her grandmother? No. Her husband? Oh, no, indeed! It was the wolf.

XXVII

A MODERN BEANSTALK

The legends of the world have been devised by timorous people. They represent the desire of man, sloshing around in a world much too big for him, to keep up his courage by whistling. He has pretended through these tales that champions of his own kind would spring up to protect him. "Let St. George do it," was a well known motto in the days of old.

And we must insist again that such tales are false and pernicious stimulants for the young. We intend to tell H. 3d that when Jack climbed up the beanstalk the giant flicked him off with one finger. We want the child to have some respect for size and to associate it with authority. Otherwise we don't see how we can possibly prevail upon him to pay any attention when we say, "Stop that." If he goes on with these fairy stories he will merely measure us coolly for a slingshot.

As a matter of fact, he doesn't pay any attention now. The time for propaganda is already here. In our stories the ogre is going to receive his due. Of course, we will add a moral. It would be wrong to lead the boy to believe that brute force is the only effective power in the world. Now and then a giant will be killed, but it will not be any easy victory

134

for one presumptuous champion with a magic sword. Instead we will explain that little Jack was not killed when the giant flipped him off the beanstalk. The huge finger struck him only a glancing blow. Nevertheless, it took Jack a good many days to get well again. It was a fine lesson for him. During his convalescence (naturally we will have to think up a shorter word) he did a lot of thinking. As soon as he was up and around he scoured the country for other boys and at last he managed to recruit a band of fifty. The first dark night Jack climbed the beanstalk again, but he took along the fifty. By a prearranged plan they fell upon the giant from all sides and managed to bear him down and kill him. We certainly are not going to admit that a giant can be opened by anything less than Jacks or better.

Following the account of the death of the giant will come the moral. We will explain that Jack is small and weak and that there are great and monstrous powers in the world which are too strong for him. But he need not wait for the superman or the magic lamp or anything like that. He must make common cause with his kind. At this point we shall probably digress for a while to go into a brief but adequate exposition of the League of Nations, municipal ownership, profit sharing and the single tax.

Dropping the serious side of the discussion, we shall add that even a great broth of a man can be spoiled by too many cooks. There is no power in the world great enough to resist the will of man if only he moves against it valiantly—and in numbers.

Maybe H. 3d will not like our version of "Jack

135

and the Beanstalk" half as well as the original. But we fear that when he grows up he is going to find that there are still dragons and ogres and assorted monsters roaming the world. We want him to be instrumental in killing them. We don't want him to get clawed by going forward in foolishly overconfident forays.

There is the Tammany Tiger, for instance. Here and there a brave young fellow rises up and says, "I'm going to kill the Tiger." Having read the fairy stories, he thinks that the thing can be done by a little courage mixed with magic. He paints RE-FORM on a banner, charges ahead before anybody but the Tiger is ready and gets chewed up.

This is sentimentally appealing, but it has been a singularly useless system of ridding the city of the Tiger. I want H. 3d to know better and to act not only more wisely but more successfully. Somewhere in the story I plan to work in a paraphrase of something Emerson once said. Jack's last words to his army just before climbing the beanstalk will be, "If you strike a giant you must kill him."

XXVIII

VOLSTEAD AND CONVERSATION

There is one argument in favor of Prohibition. It certainly helps to make conversation on a railroad train. In the years before Volstead we had ridden thousands of miles silently peering at the two strangers across the smoking compartment and wondering how to get them talking. The weather is overrated as a common starting point. It dies after a sentence.

Now we have a sure method. Begin with, "Well, this is certainly just the day for a little shot of something," and you will find enough conversation on hand to carry you across the continent. Indeed, nothing but an ocean can stop it.

Some day, of course, we are going to run into a stranger who will reply, "Prohibition is now the national law of our land and I want you to know, sir, that I intend to respect it."

This has never happened yet. It makes us wonder how the drys get from point to point. Either they stay at home, abstain from smoking or betray their cause for the sake of friendliness. During two years of frequent travel we have never yet met an advocate of Prohibition in a smoking compartment.

There was nothing but the most fiery opposition on the part of the man who was going to Rochester.

"It's making criminals out of us," he declared severely but with an ill concealed joy at the thought of being at last, in ripe middle age, a law-breaker. He carried us into Albany with tales of men who "never touched a drop until they went and passed that there law." All these belated roisterers he pictured as reeling in and out of his office under the visible effects of illegal stimulation. He sought to create the impression that he thought the condition terrible, but evidently it had contributed a new and exciting factor to the wholesale fruit business. Even the pre-Volstead drinkers he seeemed to find not unworthy of his concern. All of them used to take just one and stop. Now his life was beset with roaring graybeards.

Leaving Albany, the young man in the check suit took up the talk and began a vivid account of recent experiences in Malone, N. Y., which he identified as the strategic point in bootlegging activities. Opening on a note of pathos, in which he wrung the hearts of his hearers by recounting the amazingly low price of Scotch near the border, he introduced a merrier mood by relating a conversation between two farmers of the section which he had overheard.

"What style of car have you got?" asked one of the men in the allegedly veracious anecdote.

"Twenty cases," replied the other laconically.

According to the estimate of the narrator, a bootlegger passes through Malone every eight minutes. He saw one take a turn into Main Street careening along at fifty miles an hour and skid so dangerously that the auto tipped, throwing a case of whiskey clear across the road. "He went out of town making seventy," added the story teller.

Invariably the bootlegger was the hero of his tales. These modern Robin Hoods he pictured as little brothers to all the world except the revenue officers. Once two revenooers caught one of the gallant company and were about to proceed with him to Syracuse, toting along four telltale barrels of rye. But they had gone only a short distance on their journey when they were overtaken by two men in a motor truck escorting a prisoner, heavily manacled, and ten barrels of whiskey. After a short confab they agreed to relieve the revenuers of their prisoner and deliver both miscreants to the proper authorities in Syracuse. The gullible agents of the law gave up their man.

"And," continued the rum romancer, "they never did show up at Syracuse at all. That second crowd they weren't revenue men at all. They were bootleggers."

Indeed, the young man declared that in Northern New York there is a well organized Bootleggers' Union, which pays all fines out of a common fund. So great was his seeming admiration for the rum runners that we suspected him of being himself a member in good standing, but soon we were moved to identify him as a participant in a trade still more sinister. An acquaintance came past the green curtain and inquired eagerly, "Did you sell her?"

"Twice," said the young man enthusiastically and without regard to our look of horror as we were moved by circumstantial evidence to believe him not only a white slaver but a dishonest one.

"Yes," he continued. "I had my work cut out. You see he doesn't like Nazimova."

We were a little sorry to find that the young man was a motion picture salesman. It made us fear that perhaps some of his bootlegging yarns had been colored with the ready fiction of his business. Still it was interesting to sit and learn that Niagara Falls got "Camille" for only $300.

The middle-aged man, the one with the large acquaintance among belated drunkards, seemingly had little interest when the conversation turned from bootlegging to the silver screen. We never did hear what business "The Sheik" did in Albany because he was roaring at a skeptic about cabbage.

"I tell you," he shouted, "they got 110 tons off of every acre."

Now we yield to no man in love of cabbage, but we should not find such quantities appealing. It would compel corn beef commitments beyond the point of comfort.

The skeptic made some timid observation about onions. We did not catch whether it was for or against.

"Do you know," said the cabbage king, "that 75 per cent. of all the onions in America are eaten by Jews?" He said it with rancor, whether racial or vegetable we could not determine. To us it seemed an unusual tribute to an ancient people. No other story of their executive capacity had ever seemed to us quite so convincing. We marveled at the extraor-

140

dinary coöperation which could hold a habit so precisely to an average easy to compute and remember.

We were also moved to admiration for the census takers. Statistics seem to us man's supreme triumph in solving the mysteries of a chaotic world. Creation, of course, was divine, but even that did not involve bookkeeping.

For a time we considered abandoning our project to write a novel about a newspaper man and his son and make it, instead, a pastoral about a hero simple and sincere whose life was dedicated to the task of determining the ultimate destination of every onion raised in America. Then, since art ought to be international, we planned to widen the scope of the tale and include Bermuda. This would enable us to develop a tropical love interest and get a sex appeal into the story. We are not sure that a book would have a wide sale on onions alone.

Of course other vegetables might enter the story. There could be a villain forever tempting the hero to abandon his career and go after parsnips. Titles simply flooded our mind. We thought of "Desperate Steaks," "Out of the Frying Pan" and "A Bed of Onions," although we had a vague impression that W. L. George had done something of this sort in one of his earlier novels. "Breath Control" we dismissed as too frivolous. "Smothered" was too sensational.

Eventually we abandoned the whole project. We feared that we might not be up to the atmosphere of an onion novel.

Still, the advertising might be very effective if the

publisher could be induced to bill the book under a great, flaring headline, "The Onion Forever."

But the train of thought was cut short when the demon vegetable statistician got up and said, "If I could have just one wish in the world, I'd choose a fruit farm between here and Lockport." Looking up to see where "here" was, we observed the Rochester station. The trip had seemed but a moment, and all because of Prohibition.

By the way, did you know that 14.72 per cent. of all the potatoes raised in America come from Maine?

XXIX

LIFE, THE COPY CAT

Every evening when dusk comes in the Far West, little groups of men may be observed leaving the various ranch houses and setting out on horseback for the moving picture shows. They are cowboys and they are intent on seeing Bill Hart in Western stuff. They want to be taken out of the dull and dreary routine of the world in which they live.

But somehow or other the films simply cannot get very far away from life, no matter how hard or how fantastically they try. As we have suggested, the cowboy who struts across the screen has no counterpart in real life, but imitation is sure to bridge the gap. Young men from the cattle country, after much gazing at Hart, will begin to be like him. The styles which the cowboys are to wear next year will be dictated this fall in Hollywood.

It has generally been recognized that life has a trick of taking color from literature. Once there were no flappers and then F. Scott Fitzgerald wrote "This Side of Paradise" and created them in shoals. Germany had a fearful time after the publication of Goethe's "Werther" because striplings began to contract the habit of suicide through the influence of the book and went about dying all over the place.

143

And all Scandinavia echoed with slamming doors for years just because Ibsen sent Nora out into the night. In fact the lock on that door has never worked very well since. When "Uncle Tom's Cabin" was written things came to such a pass that a bloodhound couldn't see a cake of ice without jumping on it and beginning to bay.

If authors and dramatists can do so much with their limited public, think of the potential power of the maker of films, who has his tens of thousands to every single serf of the writing man. The films can make us a new people and we rather think they are doing it. Fifteen years ago Americans were contemptuous of all Latin races because of their habit of talking with gestures. It was considered the part of patriotic dignity to stand with your hands in your pockets and to leave all expression, if any, to the voice alone.

Watch an excited American to-day and you will find his gestures as sweeping as those of any Frenchman. As soon as he is jarred in the slightest degree out of calm he immediately begins to follow subconscious promptings and behave like his favorite motion picture actor. Nor does the resemblance end necessarily with mere externals. Hiram Johnson, the senator from California, is reported to be the most inveterate movie fan in America, and it is said that he never takes action on a public question without first asking himself, "What would Mary Pickford do under similar circumstances?" In other words the senator's position on the proposal to increase the import tax on nitrates may be traced directly to the

144

fact that he spent the previous evening watching "Little Lord Fauntleroy."

Even the speaking actors, most contemptuous of all motion picture critics, are slaves of the screen. At an audible drama in a theater the other day we happened to see a young actor who had once given high promise of achievement in what was then known as the legitimate. Eventually he went into motion pictures, but now he was back for a short engagement. We were shocked to observe that he tried to express every line he uttered with his features and his hands regardless of the fact that he had words to help him. He spoke the lines, but they seemed to him merely incidental. We mean that when his part required him to say, "It is exactly nineteen minutes after two," he tried to do it by gestures and facial expression. This is a difficult feat, particularly as most young players run a little fast or a little slow and are rather in need of regulating. When the young man left the theater at the close of the performance we sought him out and reproached him bitterly on the ground of his bad acting.

"Where do you get that stuff?" we asked.

"In the movies," he admitted frankly enough.

There was no dispute concerning facts. We merely could not agree on the question of whether or not it was true that he had become a terrible actor. Life came into the conversation. Something was said by somebody (we can't remember which one of us originated it) about holding the mirror up to nature. The actor maintained that everyday common folk talked and acted exactly like characters in the movies

145

whenever they were stirred by emotion. We made a bet and it was to be decided by what we observed in an hour's walk. At the southwest corner of Thirty-seventh street and Third avenue, we came upon two men in an altercation. One had already laid a menacing hand upon the coat collar of the other. We crowded close. The smaller man tried to shake himself loose from the grip of his adversary. And he said, "Unhand me." He had met the movies and he was theirs.

The discrepancy in size between the two men was so great that my actor friend stepped between them and asked, "What's all this row about?" The big man answered: "He has spoken lightly of a woman's name."

That was enough for us. We paid the bet and went away convinced of the truth of the actor's boast that the movies have already bent life to their will. At first it seemed to us deplorable, but the longer we reflected on the matter the more compensations crept in.

Somehow or other we remembered a tale of Kipling's called "The Finest Story In The World," which dealt with a narrow-chested English clerk, who, by some freak or other, remembered his past existences. There were times when he could tell with extraordinary vividness his adventures on a Roman galley and later on an expedition of the Norsemen to America. He told all these things to a writer who was going to put them into a book, but before much material had been supplied the clerk fell in love with a girl in a tobacconist's and suddenly forgot all his

146

previous existences. Kipling explained that the lords of life and death simply had to step in and close the doors of the past as soon as the young man fell in love because love-making was once so much more glorious than now that we would all be single if only we remembered.

But love-making is likely to have its renaissance from now on since the movies have come into our lives. Douglas Fairbanks is in a sense the rival of every young man in America. And likewise no young woman can hope to touch the fancy of a male unless she is in some ways more fetching than Mary Pickford. In other words, pace has been provided for lovers. For ten cents we can watch courtship being conducted by experts. The young man who has been to the movies will be unable to avail himself of the traditional ineptitude under such circumstances. Once upon a time the manly thing to do was mumble and make a botch of it. The movies have changed all that. Courtship will come to have a technique. A young man will no more think of trying to propose without knowing how than he would attempt a violin concert without ever having practiced. The phantom rivals of the screen will be all about him. He must win to himself something of their fire and gesture. Love-making is not going to be as easy as it once was. Those who have already wed before the competition grew so acute should consider themselves fortunate. Consider for instance the swain who loves a lady who has been brought up on the picture plays of Bill Hart. That young man who hopes to supplant the shadow idol will have to be able to shoot Indians at all ranges from four hundred yards up, and to ride one hundred thousand miles without once forgetting to keep his face to the camera.

XXX

The entire orthodox world owes a debt to Benny.
Leonard. In all the other arts, philosophies, religions
and what nots conservatism seems to be crumbling before the attacks of the radicals. A stylist may generally be identified to-day by his bloody nose. Even
in Leonard's profession of pugilism the correct
method has often been discredited of late.

It may be remembered that George Bernard Shaw
announced before "the battle of the century" that
Carpentier ought to be a fifty to one favorite in the
betting. It was the technique of the Frenchman which
blinded Shaw to the truth. Every man in the world
must be in some respect a standpatter. The scope
of heresy in Shaw stops short of the prize ring. His
radicalism is not sufficiently far reaching to crawl
through the ropes. When Carpentier knocked out
Beckett with one perfectly delivered punch he also
jarred Shaw. He knocked him loose from some of
his cynical contempt for the conventions. Mr. Shaw
might continue to be in revolt against the well-made
play, but he surrendered his heart wholly to the properly executed punch.

But Carpentier, the stylist, fell before Dempsey,

149

the mauler, in spite of the support of the intellectuals.
It seemed once again that all the rules were wrong.
Benny Leonard remains the white hope of the orthodox. In lightweight circles, at any rate, old-fashioned
proprieties are still effective. No performer in any
art has ever been more correct than Leonard. He
follows closely all the best traditions of the past.
His left hand jab could stand without revision in
any textbook. The manner in which he feints, ducks,
sidesteps and hooks is unimpeachable. The crouch
contributed by some of the modernists is not in the
repertoire of Leonard. He stands up straight like a
gentleman and a champion and is always ready to hit
with either hand.

His fight with Rocky Kansas at Madison Square
Garden was advertised as being for the lightweight
championship of the world. As a matter of fact much
more than that was at stake. Spiritually, Saint-
Saens, Brander Matthews, Henry Arthur Jones,
Kenyon Cox, and Henry Cabot Lodge were in Benny
Leonard's corner. His defeat would, by implication,
have given support to dissonance, dadaism, creative
evolution and bolshevism. Rocky Kansas does nothing according to rule. His fighting style is as form-
less as the prose of Gertrude Stein. One finds a de-
lightfully impromptu quality in Rocky's boxing.
Most of the blows which he tries are experimental.
There is no particular target. Like the young poet
who shot an arrow into the air, Rocky Kansas tosses
off a right hand swing every once and so often and
hopes that it will land on somebody's jaw.

But with the opening gong Rocky Kansas tore into
150

Leonard. He was gauche and inaccurate but terribly· persistent. The champion jabbed him repeatedly with a straight left which has always been considered the proper thing to do under the circumstances. Somehow or other it did not work. Leonard might as well have been trying to stand off a rhinoceros with a feather duster. Kansas kept crowding him. In the first clinch Benny's hair was rumpled and a moment later his nose began to bleed. The incident was a shock to us. It gave us pause and inspired a sneaking suspicion that perhaps there was something the matter with Tennyson after all. Here were two young men in the ring and one was quite correct in everything which he did and the other was all wrong. And the wrong one was winning. All the enthusiastic Rocky Kansas partisans in the gallery began to split infinitives to show their contempt for Benny Leonard and all other stylists. Macaulay turned over twice in his grave when Kansas began to lead with his right hand.

But traditions are not to be despised. Form may be just as tough in fiber as rebellion. Not all the steadfastness of the world belongs to heretics. Even though his hair was mussed and his nose bleeding, Benny continued faithful to the established order. At last his chance came. The young child of nature who was challenging for the championship dropped his guard and Leonard hooked a powerful and entirely orthodox blow to the conventional point of the jaw. Down went Rocky Kansas. His past life flashed before him during the nine seconds in which he remained on the floor and he wished that he had been

151

more faithful as a child in heeding the advice of his boxing teacher. After all, the old masters did know something. There is still a kick in style, and tradition carries a nasty wallop.

XXXI

WITH A STEIN ON THE TABLE

Half a League would be better than one. Perhaps a quarter section would be still better. The thing that sank Mr. Wilson's project, so far as America was concerned, was the machinery. It was too heavy. Not so much was needed. The only essential thing was a large round table and a pleasant room held under at least one year's lease. Of course, it should have been the right sort of table. If they had put knives and forks and, better yet, glasses upon the one in Paris, instead of ink and paper, we might already have a better world. Beer and light wines can settle subjects which defy all the subtleties possible to ink.

What the world needs, then, is not so much a league as an international beer night to be held at regular intervals by representatives of the nations. Good beer and enough of it would have settled the whole problem of the covenants which were going to be open and did not turn out that way. The little meetings would have a persuasive privacy, and yet they would not be secret to any destructive extent. An alert reporter hanging about the front door could not fail to hear the strains of "He's a jolly good fellow" drifting down the stairs from the conference room

153

and, if he were a journalist of any ability, he would have no difficulty in surmising that the crowd was entertaining the delegate from Germany and discussing indemnities.

Some persons were not quite fair in criticizing the shortcomings of President Wilson at Paris. It was easy to seize upon "open covenants" and to demolish his sincerity by pointing out the secrecy with which negotiations were carried on. It is sentimentally satisfying to every liberal and radical in the world to declare that all the walls should have come down and to continue this criticism by suggesting that the Arms conference ought to have been taken out of the Pan American Building and transferred to Tex Rickard's arena on Boyle's Thirty Acres, or the Yale Bowl. The notion is fascinating because it permits the possibility of cheering sections and enables one to picture Henry Cabot Lodge leaping to his feet every now and again and asking all the men with the R. R. banners (Reactionary Republicans) to join him in nine long rahs for the freedom of the seas. The delegates, of course, would be numbered so that the spectators could tell who was doing the kicking.

It is appealing and we wish it could be done that way, but it is not sound. We all know how bitter and destructive are legal battles which have their first hearing in the newspapers. We also remember how tenacious have been many of the struggles between capital and labor just so long as the leaders of either side were talking to each other across eight-column headlines instead of a table.

One may counter by calling to mind various evil

things which have come to the world from the tops
of tables, but we must insist again upon stressing
the point that these were not tables which supported
food and drink. In Paris various points were lost
to democracy because the supporters of the right were
outstayed by the champions of evil. In our little club
room it would be hard to put such pressure upon
anybody. He would need to do no more than shout
for the waiter to fill up his mug again and intrench
himself for the evening. The most attractive thing
about our suggestion is that though it sounds like
frivolous foolery it actually is nothing of the sort.
We are willing to accept modifications, but the scheme
would work. We have seen the pacifying effects of
food and drink upon warring factions too many times
not to respect them.

Once, at a dinner we heard Max Eastman talk
across a table to Judge Gary and both enjoyed it.
We do not mean to suggest that the two men arose
with all their previous ideas of the conduct of the
world changed. Judge Gary did not offer, in spite
of the eloquence of Eastman, to curtail the working
day in the mills of the United States Steel Company,
nor did the editor of *The Liberator* promise that thereafter he would be more kindly disposed in writing
about universal military training. But both men were
disposed to listen. Gary did not rush to the telephone to summon a Federal attorney, and there was
no disposition on the part of Eastman to call the proletariat up into immediate arms. The most friendly
thing which anybody ever said about Mr. Wilson's
League of Nations came from those opponents of the

scheme who called it "nothing but a debating society."

Talk is lint for the wounds of the world. The guns cannot begin until the statesmen have had their say. Any device which provides a pleasant place and an audience for the orators in power is distinctly a move to end war. The trouble with ultimatums is not only that they are ugly but that they are short. If certain gentlemen from Serbia could have been brought face to face with other gentlemen from Austria and empowered to thrash it out the dispute between the two nations would by no means be settled by now, but it would still be in a talking stage.

Arguments must be fostered and preserved. It may be a little tiresome to hear premiers saying, "Is that so?" to one another, but the satisfaction derived from such exchanges is enough to keep the conflicting parties from seeking a blood restoration of national egos. Food and drink are not only the greatest instigators but the best preservers of free speech in the world. Undoubtedly everybody in his time has heard some toastmaster or other insult a prominent citizen a few feet away in a manner which would be unsafe on the public highway and nothing has happened. It has been passed off as something wholly suitable to the occasion. As we listened to Max Eastman talk across the table to Judge Gary we wondered whether anybody would have even thought for a moment of sending Debs to jail if he had only had the good fortune to talk from behind a barricade of knives and forks. These are the ultimate and most effective weapons of all peaceful men. With one

156

of each in front of him even a revolutionist may bare his heart and still be safe from the bayonets of the military.

Of course, the value of the weapons is not unknown to the conservatives as well. Many a rampant reformer has gone to Washington and has seen his ideals drown one by one before his eyes in the soup. For years England managed to muddle along with Ireland by inviting nationalists out to dinner. With the spread and development of civilization the price of pottage has gone up. To-day we can afford to laugh at poor ignorant and deluded Jacob who let his pottage go for a mess of birthright.

In the light of these admissions it would be impossible to contend that all the ills of the world could be solved by the device of international beer nights. Even well fed men are not perfect. Alcohol is benign, but it does not canonize. Schemes would go on even over demitasses. There would be stratagems and surprises. And yet to our mind the stratagem, even of a statesman, can never be so potent for harm in the world as the stratagem of a general. Diplomacy is an evil game, chiefly because it has been so exclusive. Our little club would be large enough to admit all the delegates of the world. The only house rule would be "No checks cashed."

We have no idea that the heart of man is not more important than his stomach. The world will not be made over more closely to the heart's desire until we are of a better breed. But while we are waiting, friendly talks about a table may count for something. We might manage to swap a groaning world for a groaning board. There is sanction for hope in the words of the song. We know, don't we, that it's always fair weather when good fellows get together with a stein on the table. All America needs, then, to make the world safer for democracy is the stein and the good fellows.

XXXII

ART FOR ARGUMENT'S SAKE

All editors are divided into two parts. In one group are those who think that anybody who can make a good bomb can undoubtedly fashion a great sonnet. The members of the other class believe that if a man loves his country he is necessarily well fitted to be a book reviewer.

As a matter of fact, new terminology is coming into the business of criticism. A few years ago the critic who was displeased with a book called it "sensational" or "sentimental" or something like that. To-day he would voice his disapproval by writing "Pro-German" or "Bolshevist." Authors are no longer evaluated in terms of æsthetics, but rather from the point of view of political economy. Indeed, to-day we have hardly such a thing as good writers and bad writers. They have become instead either "sound" or "dangerous." A sound author is one with whose views you are in agreement.

So tightly are the lines drawn that the criticism of the leading members of each side can be accurately predicted in advance. Show me the cover of a war novel, and let me observe that it is called "The Great Folly," and I will guarantee to foreshadow with a high degree of accuracy just what the critic of The New York *Times* will say about it and also the critic of *The Liberator*. Even if it happened to be called "The Glory of Shrapnel," the guessing would be just as easy.

The manner in which anybody says anything now whether in prose, verse, music or painting is entirely secondary in the minds of all critical publications. Reviewers look for motives. Symphonies are dismissed as seditious, and lyrics are closely scanned to see whether or not their rhythms are calculated to upset the established order without due recourse to the ballot. Nor has this particular reviewer any intention of suggesting that such activity is entirely vain and fanciful. He remembers that only a month ago he began a thrilling adventure story called "The Lost Peach Pit," only to discover, when he was half through, that it was a tract in favor of a higher import duty on potash.

A vivid novel about the war by John Dos Passos has been issued under the title "Three Soldiers." One of the chief characters was a creative musician who broke under the rigor of army discipline which was repugnant to him. Nobody who wrote about the book undertook to discuss whether or not the author had painted a persuasive picture of the struggle in the soul of a credible man. Instead they argued as to just what proportion of men in the American army were discontented, and the final critical verdict is being withheld until statistics are available as to how many of them were musicians. Those who disliked the book did not speak of Mr. Dos Passos as either a realist or a romanticist. They simply called him a traitor and let it go at that. The enthusiasts on the

160

other side neglected to say anything about his style because they needed the space to suggest that he ought to be the next candidate for president from the Socialist party.

Speaking as a native-born American (Brooklyn— 1888) who once voted for a Socialist for membership in the Board of Aldermen, the writer must admit that he has found the radical solidarity of critical approval or dissent more trying than that of the conservatives. Again and again he has found, in *The Liberator* and elsewhere, able young men, who ought to know better, praising novels for no reason on earth except that they were radical. If the novelist said that life in a middlewestern town was dreary and evil he was bound to be praised by the socialist reviewers. On the other hand, any author who found in this same middle west a community or an individual not hopelessly stunted in mind and in morals, was immediately scourged as a viciously sentimental observer who had probably been one of the group which fixed upon the nomination of President Harding late at night behind the locked doors of a little room in a big hotel.

The enthusiasm of the radical critics extends not only to rebels against existing governmental principles and moral conventions, but to all those who dare to write in any new manner. There seems to be a certain confusion whereby free verse is held to be a movement in the direction of free speech.

Novels which begin in the middle and work first forward and then back, win favor as blows against the bourgeois idea that a straight line is the shortest

161

distance between two points. Of course, the radical
author can do almost anything the conservative does
and still retain the admiration of his fellows by dint
of a very small amount of tact. Rhapsodies on love
will be damned as sentimental if the author has been
injudicious enough to allow his characters to marry,
but he can retain exactly the same language if he
is careful to add a footnote that nothing is contem-
plated except the freest of free unions. A few works
are praised by both sides because each finds a different interpretation for the same set of facts. Thus,
the authors of "Dulcy" were surprised to find themselves warmly greeted in one of the Socialist dailies
as young men who had struck a blow for government
ownership of all essential industries merely because
they had introduced a big business man into their
play and, for the purposes of comic relief, had made
him a fool.

Class consciousness has become so acute that it
extends even beyond the realms of literature and
drama into the field of sports. The recent "battle of
the century" eventually simmered down into the
minds of many as a struggle between the forces of
reaction and revolution. It was known before the
fight that Carpentier would wear a flowered silk
bathrobe into the ring, while Dempsey would be clad
in an old red sweater. How could symbolism be more
perfect? Anybody who believed that Carpentier's
right would be good enough to win, was immediately
set down as a profiteer in munitions who would undoubtedly welcome the outbreak of another war.
Likewise it was unsafe to express the opinion that

Dempsey's infighting might be too much for the Frenchman, lest one be identified with the little willful group of pacifists who impeded the progress of the war. Eventually, the startling revelation was made by the reporter of a morning newspaper that he had seen Carpentier smelling a rose. After that, any belief in the invader's prowess laid whoever expressed it open to the charge, not only of aristocracy, but of degeneracy as well. After Dempsey's blows wore down his opponent and defeated him, it was generally felt by his supporters that the eight-hour day was safe, and that the open shop would never be generally accepted in America.

The only encouraging feature in the increasingly sharp feeling of class consciousness among critics is a growing frankness. Reviewers are willing to admit now that they think so and so's novel is an indifferent piece of work because he speaks ill of conscription and they believe in it. A year or so ago they would have pretended that they did not like it because the author split some infinitives.

One of the frankest writing men we ever met is the editor of a Socialist newspaper. "Whenever there's a big strike," he explained to me, "I always tell the man who goes out on the story, 'Never see a striker hit a scab. Always see the scab hit the striker.' "

"You see," he went on, "there are seven or eight other newspapers in town who will see it just the other way and I've got to keep the balance straight."

There used to be a practice somewhat similar to this among baseball umpires. Whenever the man

163

behind the plate felt that he had called a bad ball
a strike, he would bide his time until the next good
one came over and that he would call a ball. The
practice was known as "evening up" and it is no
longer considered efficient workmanship. That is, not
among umpires. The radical editor was not in the
least abashed when I quoted to him the remark of
a man who said that he always read his paper with
great interest because he invariably found the editorial opinions in the news and the news on the editorial page. "That's just what I'm trying to do," he
exclaimed delightedly. "I'm not trying to give the
people the news. I'm trying to make new Socialists
every day."

It is to be feared that even those writers who have
the opportunity to be more deliberate than the jour-
nalists have been struck with the idea that by words
they can shape the world a little closer to the heart's
desire. Throughout the war we were told so constantly that battles could be decided and ships built
and wars decided by the force of propaganda, that
every man with a portable typewriter in his suitcase
began to think of it as a baton. There was a day
when a novelist was satisfied if he could capture a
little slice of life and get it between the covers of
his book. Now everybody writes to shake the world.
The smell of propaganda is unmistakable.

With literature in its present state of mind critics
cannot be expected to watch and wait for the great
American novel or the great American play. Instead
they look for the book which made the tariff possible,
or the play which ended the steel strike.

XXXIII

Richard Le Gallienne was lamenting, once, that he probably would never be able to write a best-seller like Hall Caine or Marie Corelli. "It's no use," he said. "You can't fake it. Bad writing is a gift."

So is college spirit. That is why almost all the plays and motion pictures about football games and hazing and such like are so fearfully unconvincing. Nobody who is hired for money can possibly make the same joyful ass of himself as a collegian under strictly amateur momentum. Expense has not been spared, nor pains, in the building of "Two Minutes To Go," with the delightful Charlie Ray, but it just isn't real. Films may be faithful enough in depicting such trifling emotions as hate and passion and mother-love, but the feeling which animates the freshman when Yale has the ball on the three-yard line is something a little too searing and sacred for the camera's eye.

One of the difficulties of catching any of this spirit for play or for picture is that there is no logical reason for its existence. Logic won't touch it. The director and his entire staff would all have to be inspired to be able to make a college picture actually glow. There is not that much inspiration in all Hollywood.

165

PIECES OF HATE

The partisanship of the big football games has always been to me one of the most mystifying features in American life. It is all the more mystifying from the fact that it grips me acutely twice a year when Harvard plays Princeton, and again when we play Yale. I find no difficulty in being neutral about Bates of Middlebury. It did not even worry me much when Georgia scored a touchdown. The encounters with Yale and Princeton are not games but ordeals. Of course, there is no sense to it. A victory for Harvard or a defeat makes no striking difference in the course of my life. My job goes on just the same and the servants will stay, and there will be a furnace and food even if the Crimson is defeated by many touchdowns.

I never played on a Harvard eleven, nor even had a relative on any of the teams. There was a second cousin on the scrub, but he was before my time, and it cannot be that all my interest has been drummed up by his career. I don't know the coaches nor the players. Yale and Princeton have not wronged me. In fact, I once sold an article to a Yale man who is now conducting a magazine in New York. Naturally it was on a neutral subject, which happened to be the question of whether mothers were any more skillful than fathers in handling children. Orange and black are beautiful colors and "Old Nassau" is a stirring tune. Woodrow Wilson meant well at Paris, and Big Bill Edwards was as pleasant-spoken a collector of income taxes as I ever expect to meet.

Yet all this is forgotten when the teams run out

on to the gridiron. I find myself yelling "Block that kick! Block that kick! Block that kick!" or "Touchdown! Touchdown!" as if my heart would break. It is pretty lucky that the old devil who bought Faust's soul has never come along and tempted me in the middle of a football game. He could drive a good bargain cheap. There have been times when for nothing more than a five yard gain through the center of the line he could have had not only my soul, but a third mortgage on the house. If he played me right he might even get that recipe for making near beer closer.

The strangest part of all this is that the emotions described are not exceptional. A number of sane persons have assured me that they feel just the same about the big games. One of my best friends in college was always known to us as "the brother of the man who dropped the punt." The man who actually committed that dire deed was not even mentioned. I remember, also, a Harvard captain whose team lost and who horrified the entire university by remarking at the team dinner a few weeks later that he was always going to look back on the season with pleasure because he thought that he and the rest of the players had had good fun, even though they had lost to Yale. Naturally he was never allowed to return to Cambridge after his graduation. His unfortunate remark came a few years before the passage of the sedition law, but there was a militant public opinion in the college fully capable of taking care of such cases.

Feeling, then, as I do, that there is no such poignant ordeal possible to man as sitting through a tight Harvard-Yale game, any screen story of football seems not only piffling but sacrilegious. In the Charlie Ray picture, the two contending teams were Stanley and Baker. There were views of the rival cheering sections and closer ones of Charlie Ray running the length of the gridiron for a touchdown. This feat was made somewhat easy for him by the fact that all the extra people engaged for the picture seemed to have been instructed to slap him lightly above the knee with the little finger of the right hand and then fall upon their faces so that he might step over them.

It was not this palpable artificiality which was the most potent factor in bringing me into an extreme state of calm. A long Harvard run made possible by the entire Yale team's being struck by lightning would seem to me thoroughly satisfactory. The trouble with "Two Minutes To Go" was that I never forgot for a moment that Charlie Ray was a motion picture star instead of a halfback. Of course, you might object that I should properly have the same feeling when seeing Ray in pictures where he is engaged in altercations with holdup men and other scoundrels. That is different. In such situations the stratagems of the films are amply convincing, but in football nobody can possibly play the villain so effectively as a Yaleman. We have often wondered how one university could possibly corner the entire supply of treacherous and beetle-browed humanity.

The foemen lined up against Charlie Ray didn't begin to be fierce enough. Nor did the rival groups of rooters serve any better to convince me of their authenticity. It was quite evident that they were

swayed by no emotion other than that of a willing-
ness to obey the orders of the director. Football is
too warm and passionate a thing to be reduced to the
flat dimensions of the screen. Battle, murder, sudden death and many other things are done amply well
in films. Football is different. Though it injure the
heart, increase the blood pressure and shorten life,
only the reality will do.

XXXIV

"ATABOY!"

Thomas Burke has a cultivated taste for low life and he records his delight in Limehouse so vividly that it is impossible to doubt his sincerity. In his volume of essays called "Out and About London," he spreads his enthusiasm over the entire "seven hundred square miles of London, in which adventure is shyly lurking for those who will seek her out."

In the spreading there is at least ground for suspicion that here and there authentic enthusiasm has worn a bit thin. It is no more than a suspicion, for Burke is a skillful writer who can set an emotion to galloping without showing the whip. Only when he comes to describe a baseball game is the American reader prepared to assert roundly that Burke is merely parading an enthusiasm which he does not feel. We could not escape the impression that the English author felt that a baseball game was the most primitive thing America had to offer and that he was in duty bound to enthuse over this exhibition of human nature in the raw.

We have seen many Englishmen at baseball games. We have even attempted to explain to a few visitors the fine points of the game, why John McGraw spoke in so menacing a manner to the umpire or why Hughie

Jennings ate grass and shouted "Ee-Yah!" at the batter. Invariably the Englishman has said that it was all very strange and all very delightful. Never have we believed him. The very essence of nationality lies in the fact that the other fellow's pastime invariably seems a ridiculous affair. One may accept the cookery, the politics and the religion of a foreign nation years before he will take an alien game to his heart. We doubt whether it would be possible to teach an American to say "Well played" in less than a couple of generations.

Burke has no fears. Not only does he describe the game in a general way, but he plunges boldly ahead in an effort to record American slang. The title of the essay is well enough. Burke calls it "Attaboy!" This is, of course, authentic American slang. It meets all the requirements, being in common use, having a definite meaning and affording a short cut to the expression of this meaning. We can not quite accept the spelling. There is, perhaps, room for controversy here. When the American army first came to France the word attracted a good deal of attention and some French philologists undertook to follow it to the source. One of them quickly discovered that he was dealing not with a word but a contracted phrase. We are of the opinion that thereafter he went astray, for he declared that "Ataboy" was a contraction of "At her boy," and he offered the freely translated substitute "Au travail garçon."

It will be observed that Mr. Burke has given his attaboy a "t" too many. "That's the boy" is the source of the word. Perhaps it would be more ac-

curately spelled if written " 'at 'a boy." The single
"a" is a neutral vowel which has come to take the
place of the missing "the." The same process has occurred in the popular phrases " 'ataswingin' " and
" 'ataworkin'." These, however, have a lesser standing. "Ataboy" is almost official. One of the American army trains which ran regularly from Paris to
Chaumont began as the Atterbury special, being
named after the general in charge of railroads. In
a week it had become the Ataboy special, and so it
remained even in official orders.

Some of the slang which Burke records as being
observed at the game is palpably inaccurate. Thus
he reports hearing a rooter shout, "Take orf that
pitcher!" It is safe to assume that what the rooter
actually said was, "Ta-ake 'im out!"

Again Burke writes, "An everlasting chorus, with
reference to the scoring board, chanted like an anthem—'Go-ing up! Go-ing up! Go-ing up!' "

Now, as a matter of fact, the "go-ing up!" did not
refer to the scoring board, but to the pitcher who must
have been manifesting signs of losing control. The
shouts of baseball crowds are so closely standardized
that we think we have a right to view with a certain
distrust such unfamiliar snatches of slang as "He's
pitching over a plate in heaven," or "Gimme some
barb' wire. I wanter knit a sweater for the barnacle
on second," and also, "Hey, catcher, quit the diamond, and lemme l'il brother teach you." It is impossible for us to reconcile "lemme l'il brother" and
"quit the diamond."

It must be said in justice to Burke that it is en-
172

tirely possible that he did hear some of the outlandish phrases which he has jotted down. Among the dough-boys gathered for the game there may have been some former college professor who had devoted the afternoon to convincing his comrades that he was no highbrow, but a typical American. Such a theory would account for "quit the diamond."

XXXV

Perseverance, courage, acumen, unceasing vigilance, hard work and application are all required of the man who would win money at the races. He should also have some capital in easily marketable securities.

During his preliminary days at the university, the man who would win money on the races should specialize in science. It will be quite impossible for him in his later career to tell whether his selection was beaten by a nose or a head, unless he is absolutely familiar with the bone structure of the horse (Equidoe), (Ungulate), (E. caballus). In freshman zoölogy he will learn that, at the highest, the teeth number forty-four, and that the horse as a domestic animal dates from prehistoric times. This will serve to explain to him the character of the entries in some of the selling races.

Geology will make it possible for him to distinguish between "track—slow" and "track—muddy." The romance languages need not be avoided. French will enable the student to ask the price on Trompe La Morte without recourse to the subterfuge of "What are you laying on the top one?" In spite of the amount of science required, the young man will find that he has small need of mathematics. A working knowledge of subtraction will suffice.

As has been well said in many a commencement address, college is not the end but merely the beginning of education. The graduate should begin his intensive preparation not later than twelve hours before going to the track. He will find that the first edition of *The Morning Telegraph* is out by midnight. Hindoo's selections are generally on page eight. I have never known the identity of Hindoo, but there is internal evidence pointing toward President Harding. At any rate, Hindoo is a man who has mastered the pre-election style of the President. His good will to all horses, black, brown and bay, is boundless.

In studying Mr. Hindoo's advice concerning the first race at Belmont Park last week, I found, "Captain Alcock—Last race seems to give him the edge." If I had gone no further, my mind might have been easy, but in chancing to look down the column I noted, "Servitor—Well suited under the conditions"; "Pen Rose—Plainly the one that is to be feared"; "Bellsolar—May be heard from if up to her last race." On such minute examination the edge of Captain Alcock seemed to grow more blunt. "Neddam," I discovered, "will bear watching," and "Hobey Baker may furnish the surprise." To a man of scientific training such conflicting testimony is disturbing. What for instance would the world have thought of the scholarship of Aristotle if, after declaring that the earth was spherical, he had added that it might be well to have a good place bet—at two to one—on its being flat.

175

As happens all too often in the swing away from science, mere emotion was allowed to rush in unimpeded. Turning to a publication called *The Daily Running Horse*, I found the section dealing with the first race to be run at Belmont Park and read, "Captain Alcock is a nice horse right now." That settled it. All too seldom in this world does one find an individual who has the edge and still refrains from slashing about with it and cutting people. Captain Alcock was represented to us as "nice" in spite of the fact that he was "in with a second rate lot," as *The Daily Running Horse* went on to state. Later it seemed to us that the boast was in bad taste, but this factor, which we recognized immediately after the running of the first race as groundless condescension, appeared at the time a rather fetching sort of democracy. Captain Alcock was willing to associate with second raters and didn't even mind admitting it.

The price was eleven to ten, and after we made our bet the bookmaker revised his figures down to nine to ten. There was a thrill in having been a party to "hammering down the price." Soon we were to wish that Captain Alcock had been much less nice. Away from the barrier he went on his journey of a mile with a lead of two lengths. Next it was four and then five. His heels threw dust upon the second raters. Around the turn came Captain Alcock flaunting his edge in every stride. As they straightened out into the stretch the man behind us remarked, "Captain Alcock will win in a common canter."

The Captain was content to do no such thing. Although in with second raters he remained a nice horse

176

and he was willing to do nothing common even for the sake of victory. He began to ease up in order to become companionable with the field. Evidently he had felt unduly conspicuous so far in front. Winning in a common canter was not cricket to his mind. He wanted to make a race of it while there was still time. And as the speed and the lead of Captain Alcock abated, down the stretch from far in the rear dashed the black mare Bellsolar. Suddenly I remembered the ominous words of Hindoo, "May be heard from if up to her last race." Evidently Bellsolar was up. Captain Alcock was carrying the business of being nice much too far. Before he could do anything about it, Bellsolar was at his shoulders. She did not stop for greeting, but dashed past and won before the genial Captain could begin sprinting again.

As a matter of fact, it was not until the next day that I appreciated just how much wisdom had been contained in *The Daily Running Horse*, advice which I had neglected. Turning back to the first race I found, "Advised play—None, too tough." If the tipster had only kept up that pace throughout the afternoon all his followers would be winners at the track.

177

XXXVI

ONE TOUCH OF SLAPSTICK

The Duchess in *Clair de Lune* implored her gentleman friend to speak to her roughly, using hedge and highroad talk. Theatrical managers have now come to realize that many of us who may never hope to be duchesses are still swayed by this back to the soil movement. The humor of musical comedy grows more robust as the season wanes. It is broader, thicker and, to my mind, funnier. Comedy, like Antæus, must keep at least a tiptoe on the earth. When the spirit of fun begins to sicken it is time that he should be hit severely with a bladder. Having been knocked down, he will rise refreshed.

All of which is preliminary to the expression of the opinion that Jim Barton, now playing at the Century, is the funniest clown who has appeared in New York this season. Mr. Barton was discovered in a burlesque show by some astute theatrical scout several seasons ago. Burlesque was several rungs higher in the ladder than his starting point, for his career included appearances in carnivals and the little shows which ply up and down some of the rivers, giving nightly performances on their boat whenever there is a cluster of light big enough to indicate a village. Jim Barton has been trained, therefore, in

178

capturing the interest and attention of primitive and unsophisticated theatergoers. This training has encouraged him in zest and violence. It has impressed upon him the conception that the fundamental appeal to all sorts of people and all sorts of intelligences is rhythm. "When in doubt, dance" is his motto.

Primarily he developed his dancing as something which should make people laugh. It was, and is, full of stunts and grotesque movements and surprising turns. But it has not remained just funny. Consciously or unconsciously he knows, just as Charlie Chaplin knows, that funny things must be savored with something else to capture interest completely. And when you watch the antics of Barton and laugh there comes unexpectedly, every now and then, a sudden tightening of the emotions as you realize that some particular pose or movement is not funny at all, but a gorgeously beautiful picture. For instance, when Barton begins his skating dance the first reaction is one of amusement. There is a recognizable burlesque of the traditional stunts of the man on ice, but that is lost presently in the further realization that the thing is amazingly skillful and graceful. Again he follows a Spanish dancer with castanets and seems to depend upon nothing more than the easy laugh accorded to the imitator, but as he goes on it isn't just a burlesque. He has captured the whole spirit and rhythm of the dance.

There is, perhaps, something of hypocrisy and swank in taking the performance of Barton and seeming to imply, "Of course I like this man because I see all sorts of things in his work that his old burlesque audiences never recognized." It is dishonest, too, because as a matter of fact I like exactly the same things which won his audiences in the old Columbia circuit. I have never been able to steel myself against the moment in which the comedian steps up behind the stout lady and slaps her resoundingly between the shoulder blades. Jim Barton is particularly good because he hits louder and harder than any other comedian I ever saw. But even for this liking a defense is possible. The influx of burlesque methods ought to have a thoroughly cleansing influence in American musical comedy. More refined entertainment has often been unpleasantly salacious, not because it was daring but because it was cowardly. Familiar stories of the smoking car and the barroom have been brought into Broadway theaters often enough, but in disguised form. They have minced into the theater. The appeal created by this form of humor has been never to the honest laugh but to the smirk. If I were a censor I think I would allow a performer to say or do almost anything in the theater if only he did it frankly and openly. The blue pencil ought to be used only against furtive things. You may not like smut, but it is never half so objectionable as shamefacedness. The best tonic I can think of for the hangdog school of musical comedy to which we have fast been drifting is the immediate importation to Broadway of fifty comedians exactly like Jim Barton. Of course, the only trouble is that the scouts would probably turn up with the report that there was not even one.

Still rumor is going about of at least one other.

ONE TOUCH OF SLAPSTICK

I am reliably informed that Bobby Clark of *Peek-A-Boo* is one of the funniest men of the year. Unfortunately I am not in a position to make a first hand report because on the night his show opened at the Columbia I was watching *Mixed Marriage* break into another theater, or attending a revival of *John Ferguson* or something like that.

Accordingly, I missed the scene in which Bobby Clark tries to put his head into the lion's mouth. Clark must be a good comedian, because he sounds funny even when you get him at second or third hand in the form, "And then you see he says, 'You do it fine. You even smell like a lion. Take off the head now and we'll get along.'"

As it has been explained to me, Clark and the other comedian are hired by a circus because the trained lion has suddenly become too ill to perform. Clark's partner is to put on a lion's skin and pretend to be a lion while Clark goes through the usual stunts of the trainer, including the feat of putting his head into the lion's mouth. At the last minute the lion recovers and is wheeled out on to the stage in a big cage. Clark believes the animal is his partner in disguise and compliments him warmly on the manner in which he roars. Finally, however, he becomes irritated when there is no response, except a roar, to his request, "Take off the head now and come on." After a second roar Clark remarks with no little pique, "Come on, now, cut it out, you're not so good as all that."

What happens after that I don't know because the people who have been to the Columbia Theater always leave you in doubt as to whether Clark actually goes into the lion's den or not. Presumably not, because later in the show, according to these reports, there is a drill by The World's Worst Zouaves in which Clark as the chief zouave whistles continually for new formations only to have nothing happen. Whether Clark is the originator of the material about the lion and the rest, or only the executor, I am not prepared to say. All the scouts talk as if he made it up as he went along, and whenever a comedian can bring about that state of mind there need be no doubt of his ability.

XXXVII

By this time, of course, we ought to know the danger signals in a novel and realize the exact spot at which to come to a full stop. On page 54 of "The Next Corner," by Kate Jordan, we found the situation in which Robert, husband, came face to face with Elsie, wife, after a separation of three years. Mining interests had called him to Burma, and she, being given the world to choose from, had decided to live in Paris. He was punctual at the end of his three years in arriving at his wife's apartment, but she was not there. The maid informed him that she had gone to a tea at the home of the Countess Longueval. Without stopping to wait for an invitation John hurried after her. He entered the huge and garish reception room and there, yes there, was Elsie. But perhaps Miss Jordan had better tell it:

"The effect she produced on him, in her yellow gauze, that though fashioned for afternoon wear was so transparent it left a good deal of her body visible, with her face undisguisedly tricked out and her gleaming cigarette poised, was a harsh one—a marionette with whom fashion was an idolatry; an over-decorated, empty eggshell. She could feel this, and in a desperate way persisted in the affectation which sustained her, the more so that under Robert's earnest gaze a feeling of guilt made her hideously uncomfortable.

" 'Throw that away,' Robert said quietly with a scant look at the cigarette."

It seemed strange to us that Robert had been so little influenced toward liberalism during his three years in Burma, for that was the spot where Kipling's soldier found the little Burmese girl "a smokin' of a whackin' big cheeroot."

Still, Robert carried his point. Elsie, our heroine, gave a laugh. What sort of a laugh, do you suppose? Quite so, "an empty laugh," and "she turned to flick it from her fingers"; that is, the cigarette. Perhaps we should add that she flicked it to "a table that held the smokers' service." Elsie, undoubtedly, had degenerated during Robert's absence, but she was still too much the lady to put ashes on the carpet. And yet she did use cosmetics. This was the second thing which Robert took up with her. In the cab he wanted to know why she put "all that stuff" on her face. Perhaps her answer was a little perplexing, for she said, "Embellishment, mon cher. Pour la beauté, pour la charme!"

"I'm quite of the world in my tolerance," he explained to her. "If you needed help of this sort and applied it delicately to your face I'd not mind. In fact, if delicately done, probably I'd not know of it."

This, of course, seems to us an immoral attitude. Things are right or wrong, whether one notices them or not. After all, the recording angel would know.

Elsie could use paint and powder with such delicacy as to deceive him. However, we are interrupting Robert, who went on, and "His voice grew kinder, although his eyes remained sternly grave."

"It's been from the beginning of the world," he said, "and it is in the East, wherever there are women. But—and make a note of it—they are always women of a certain sort."

Seemingly, Robert got away with this statement, although it is not true. Manchu women of the highest degree paint a great scarlet circle on the side of their face in spite of the fact that there is a native proverb which, freely translated, may be rendered, "Discretion is the better part of pallor."

It is only fair to add that the indiscretions of Elsie went beyond powder and paint and even beyond smoking cigarettes. When her husband told her that he must make a brief business trip to England she asked to be excused from accompanying him on the ground that she would prefer to remain in Paris for a while. As a matter of fact, she planned to go to Spain. And she did. She went to a house party at the home of Don Arturo Valda y Moncado, Marques de Burgos. She had been told that it was to be a house party, but when she got to the isolated little castle on the top of the crag she found no one but Don Arturo Valda y Moncado, Marques de Burgos. No sooner had she arrived than a storm began to rage and the last mule coach went down the mountain. She must stay the night! Still, after her first wild pleadings that he allow her to clamber down the mountain alone at night until she could find a hotel, reasonable in price and respectable, she did not feel so lonely with Arturo. To be sure, he sounded a good deal like a house party all by himself, and more than that she loved him.

After dinner he began to make love and soon she joined him. He grew impassioned, and Elsie said that she would throw in her lot with his and never leave him. In a transport of joy, Arturo was about to bestow upon her one of those Spanish kisses which no novelist can round off in less than a page and a half. Elsie commanded him to be patient. First, she said, she must write a letter to her husband. In this moment Arturo was superb in his Latin restraint. He did not suggest a cablegram or even a special delivery stamp. Perhaps it would have meant death to go to the postoffice on such a night. Elsie wrote to Robert, painstakingly and frankly, confessing that she loved Arturo and was going to remain with him and that she would not be home at all any more. Then a sure footed serving man was intrusted with the letter and told to seek a post box on the mountain side.

No sooner was that out of the way than a Spanish peasant entered the house and shot Arturo. It seems that Arturo had betrayed his daughter. The shot killed Arturo and Elsie wished she had never sent the letter. Unfortunately, you can't make your confession and eat it too. No postscript was possible. Elsie staggered down the mountain side and a chapter later she woke up in a hospital in Bordeaux. The strain had been too great.

Nor could we stand it either. We sought out somebody else who had already read the book and he told us that Elsie went back to America and found her husband, and that for months and months she lived in an agony of shame, thinking he knew all about what had never happened. Finally she decided that he didn't, and then she lived months and months in an agony of fear that the letter was still on its way. She got up every morning, opening everything feverishly and finding only bills and advertisements. At this point the person who knew the story was interrupted in telling us about it, but we think we can supply the end.

After more months and months, in which first shame died and then fear, hope was born. And then came happiness. The old hunted look faded from the eyes of Elsie. She seemed a superbly normal woman, save in one respect. During the political campaign of 1920, when practically every visitor who came to the house would remark, at one time or other during the course of the evening, "Don't you think this man Burleson is a mess?" Elsie would look up with just the suggestion of a faint smile about her fine, sensitive mouth and answer, "Oh, I don't know."

XXXVIII

ADVENTURE MADE PAINLESS

One of my favorite characters in all fiction is D'Artagnan. He was forever fighting duels with people and stabbing them, or riding at top speed over lonely roads at night to save a woman's name or something. I believe that I glory in D'Artagnan because of my own utter inability to do anything with a sword. Beyond self-inflicted razor wounds, no blood has been shed by me. Horseback riding is equally foreign to my experience, and I have done nothing for any woman's name. And why should I? D'Artagnan does all these things so much better that there is not the slightest necessity for personal muddling. When he gallops I ride too, clattering along at breakneck speed between ghostly lines of trees. Only there is no ache in my legs the next morning. Nor heartache either over heroines.

He is my substitute in adventure. After an evening with him I can go down to the office in the morning and go through routine work without the slightest annoying consciousness that it is, after all, pretty dull stuff. I am not tempted to put on my hat and coat and fling up my job in order to go out to seek adventures with swordsmen and horses and provocative ladies in black masks.

Undoubtedly there must be some longing in me for

all this or I would not have such a keen interest in *The Three Musketeers*, but, having read about it, there is no craving for actual deeds. Possibly, after a long evening with a tale of adventure, I may swagger a little the next day and puzzle a few office boys with a belligerent manner to which they are not accustomed; but they do not fit into the picture perfectly enough to maintain the mood. It has been satisfied, and when it begins to tug again there are other books which will serve to gratify my keen desire to hear the clink of blades and the sound of running footsteps on the cobbles as the miscreants give way. The scurvy knaves! The system saves time and expense and arnica. Without it I might not be altogether reconciled to Brooklyn.

In my opinion, most of the men and women whom I know find the same relief in books and plays and motion pictures. The rather stout lady on the floor below us has three small children. I imagine that they are a fearful nuisance, but recently, after getting them to bed, she has been reading "The Sheik." Her husband—he is one of these masterful men— told me that he had glanced at the book himself and found it silly and highly colored. He said that he was going to tell her to stop. I agreed with him as to the silliness of the book, but it seemed to me that his wife had earned her right to a fling on the desert. If I knew him a little better, I would go on to say that it ought to comfort him to have his wife reading such a highly flavored romance. He is excessively jealous, and he ought to be pleased to have a possibly roving fancy so completely occupied by an

189

intense interest in an Arab chieftain who never lived —no, not even in Arabia or any place at all outside the pages of a book. The husband has no need to worry. There is no one in our neighborhood who resembles Ben Ahmed Abdullah—or whatever his fool name may be.

Once, when my neighbor found me at the door of his apartment, where I had gone to borrow half an orange, he seemed unusually surly. That was certainly a groundless suspicion. At the time I was entirely absorbed in "The Outline of History." Mrs. X—of course I can't give her name or even provide any description which might serve to identify her— was entirely safe from my attentions, for during that particular week I was rather taken with Cleopatra, even though Wells did speak slightingly of her. Unfortunately we have no adequate idea of Cleopatra's appearance. Wells attempts no description. The only existing portrait is one of those conventionalized Egyptian things with the arms held out stiffly as if the siren of the Nile was trying to indicate to the clerk the size of the shoe which she desired. Still, we can imply something from the enthusiasm of Antony and the others. Somehow or other, I have always felt sure that there was not the slightest resemblance between Cleopatra and Mrs. X.

Here is what I am trying to get at. Mr. X sells something or other, and apparently nobody in New York wants it, which makes it necessary for him to go on long journeys in which he touches Providence, Boston, New Bedford, and Bangor. Practically all my evenings are spent at home.

ADVENTURE MADE PAINLESS

I have spoken of the stairs, but it is only a short flight. Mrs. X is sentimental and I am romantic. And we are both quite safe, and Mr. X can go peacefully and enthusiastically around Bangor selling whatever it is which he has to sell. I resemble the Sheik Ben Ahmed Abdullah even less than Mrs. X resembles Cleopatra. Mr. Smith (we might as well abandon subterfuges and come out frankly with the name, since I have already been indiscreet enough for him to identify the personages concerned) has no rival but a phantom one.

Realizing how much Smith and I and Mrs. Smith owe to the protecting consolations of fiction, which includes history as written by Wells, I feel that I ought to go on to generalize in favor of many much-abused types of entertainment. Whenever a youngster steals anything, or a wife runs away from home, the motion pictures are blamed. Censorship is devoted to removing all traces of bloodshed from the films. Police magistrates are called in to suppress farces dealing with folk given to high jinks, on the ground that they threaten the morals of the community. We assume, of course, that the censors are thinking of morals in terms of deeds. They can hardly be ambitious enough to hope to curtail the thoughts of a community.

And I deny their major premise. Evil instincts are in us all. Practically everybody would enjoy robbing a bank or running away with somebody with whom he ought not to run away. These lawless instincts are invariably drained off by watching their mimic presentment in novels and films and plays.

191

PIECES OF HATE

If only accurate statistics were available, I would wager and win on the proposition that not half of 1 per cent of all the cracksmen in America have ever seen *Alias Jimmy Valentine*. No burglar could watch the play without being shamed out of his job by sheer envy. An ounce of self-respect—and there are figures to show that yeggs average three and a quarter—would keep a crook from continuing in his bungling way after observing the manner in which Jimmy Valentine opens the door of a safe merely by sandpapering his fingers. What sort of person do you suppose could go and buy nitroglycerine ungrudgingly after that? Even by the least optimistic estimate of human nature, the worst we could expect from a criminal who had seen the play would be to have him make a gallant and sincere effort to employ the touch system in his own career. Such attempts would be easy to frustrate. Night watchmen could creep up on the idealists and catch them unaware. They could be traced by their cursing. And, of course, the police might keep an eye open at the doors of the sandpaper shops.

Kiki, David Belasco's adaptation from the French, taps another rich vein of human depravity and allows it to be exploited and exhausted by means of drama. The heroine of the play is a rowdy little baggage. She has a civil word for no man. The truth is not in her. Now, every child born into the world would like to lie and be impertinent. There is practically no fun in being polite, and truth-telling is most indifferent judged solely as an indoor sport. Manners and veracity are things which people

192

ADVENTURE MADE PAINLESS

learn slowly and painfully. Undoubtedly both are
useful, though I am not at all sure that their importance is not somewhat exaggerated. Community
life demands certain sacrifices, particularly as the
pressure of civilization increases. The men of a
primitive tribe do not get up in the subway to give
their seats to ladies, because they have no subways.
Likewise, having no hats, they are not obliged to take
them off. Of course it goes deeper than that. Even
a primitive civilization has weather, and yet one
seldom hears an Indian in his native state observing:
"Isn't it unusually warm for November?"

Once everybody was primitive, and the most intensive training cannot wholly obliterate the old
longing to be done with strange and self-imposed
trappings. Until it is licked out of them, children
are savagely rude. Training can alter practice, but
even the most severe chastisement cannot get deep
enough to affect an instinct. We all want to be rude,
and we would, now and again, break loose in unre-
strained spells of boorishness if it were not for an
occasional Kiki who does the work for us. Accordingly, one of the most salutary forms of entertainment is the comedy of bad manners which recurs
in our theater every once in so often.

"But," I hear somebody objecting, "no matter how
much each of us may like to be rude, we don't care
much about it when it is done to us. In real life we
would all run from Kiki because her monstrous brag-
ging would irritate us, and her vulgarity and bad
manners would be most annoying."

All that would be true but for one factor. In any

193

play which achieves success a curious transference of personality takes place. Before a play begins the audience is separated from the people on the stage by a number of barriers. First of all, there is the curtain, but by and by that goes up. The orchestra pit and the footlights still stand as moats to keep us at our distance. Then the magic of the playhouse begins to have its effect. If the actors and the playwrights know the tricks of the business, they soon lift each impressionable person from his seat and carry him spiritually right into the center of the happenings. He becomes one or more persons in the play. We do not weep when Hamlet dies because we care anything in particular about him. His death can hardly come as a surprise. We knew he was going to die. We even knew that he had been dead for a long time.

Probably a few changes have been made in adapting *Kiki* from the French. Kiki is made just a bit more respectable than she was in the French version, but she remains enough of a gamin and a rebel against taste and morals to satisfy the outlaw spirit of an American audience. She is for the New York stage "a good girl," but since this seems to be only the slightest check upon her speech and conduct, there can be no violent objection. Of course the type is perfectly familiar in the American theater, but this time it seems to us better written than usual, and much more skillfully and warmly played. Indeed, in my opinion, Miss Ulric's Kiki is the best comedy performance of the season. Even this is not quite enough. It has been a lean season, and this particular piece of acting is good enough to stand out in a brilliant one. The final scene of the play, in which Kiki apologizes for being virtuous, seems to me a truly dazzling interpretation of emotions. It is comic because it is surprising, and it is surprising because it concerns some of the true things which people neglect to discuss.

By seeing *Alias Jimmy Valentine*, the safe-cracking instinct which lies dormant in us may be satisfied. *Kiki* allows us to indulge our fondness for being rude without alienating our friends. But more missionary work remains. In *The Idle Inn*, Ben-Ami appears as a horse thief. Personally, I have no inclination in that direction. I would not have the slightest idea what to do with a horse after stealing him. My apartment is quite small and up three flights of stairs. However, there are other vices embodied in the rôle which are more appealing to me. The rôle is that of a masterful man, which has always been among my thwarted ambitions. In the second act Ben-Ami breaks through a circle of dancing villagers and, seizing the bride, carries her off to the forest. Probably New York will never realize how many weddings have been carried on without mishap this season solely because of Ben-Ami's performance in *The Idle Inn*. In addition to entrusting him with all my eloping for the year, I purpose to let Ben-Ami swagger for me. He does it superbly. To my mind this young Jewish actor is one of the most vivid performers in our theater. His silences are more eloquent than the big speeches of almost any other star on Broadway.

The play is nothing to boast about. Once it was in Yiddish, and as far as spirit goes it remains there. Once it was a language, and now it is words. The usually adroit Arthur Hopkins has fallen down badly by providing Ben-Ami with a mediocre company. He suffers like an All-America halfback playing on a scrub team. The other players keep getting in his way.

One more production may be drawn into the discussion, but only by extending the field of inquiry a little. *The Chocolate Soldier*, which is based on Shaw's *Arms and the Man*, can hardly be said to satisfy the soldiering instinct in us by a romantic tale of battle. Shaw's method is more direct. He contents himself with telling us that the only people who do get the thrill of adventure out of war are those who know it only in imagination. His perfect soldier is prosaic. It is the girl who has never seen a battle who romances about it. Still, Shaw does make it possible for us to practice one vice vicariously. After seeing a piece by him the spectator does not feel the need of being witty. He can just sit back and let George do it.

XXXIX

THE TALL VILLA

"The Tall Villa," by Lucas Malet, is a novel, but it may well serve as a textbook for those who want to know how to entertain a ghost. There need be no question that such advice is needed. For all the interest of the present generation in psychical research, we treat apparitions with scant courtesy. Suppose a visitor goes into a haunted room and at midnight is awakened by a specter who carries a bloody dagger in one hand and his ghostly head in the other; does the guest ask the ghost to put his things down and stay a while? He does not. Instead, he rushes screaming from the room or pulls the bedclothes over his head and dies of fright.

Ghosts walk because they crave society and they get precious little of it. Frances Copley, the heroine of "The Tall Villa," managed things much better. When the apparition of Lord Oxley first appeared to her she did not faint or scream. On the contrary, the author tells us, "The breeding, in which Frances Copley trusted, did not desert her now. After the briefest interval she went on playing—she very much knew not what, discords more than probably, as she afterward reflected!"

After all, Lord Oxley may have been a ghost, but

he was still a gentleman. Indeed, when she saw him
later she perceived that the shadow "had grown,
in some degree, substantial, taking on for the most
part, definite outline, definite form and shape. That,
namely, of a young man of notably distinguished
bearing, dressed (in as far as, through the sullen
evening light, Frances could make out) in clothes of
the highest fashion, though according to a long dis-
carded coloring and cut."

From friends of the family Frances learned that
young Oxley, who had been dead about a century
and a half, had shot himself on account of unrequited
love. After having looked him up and found that
he was an eligible ghost in every particular, Frances
decided to take him up. She continued to play for
him without the discords. In fact, she began to look
forward to his afternoon calls with a great deal of
pleasure. Her husband did not understand her. She
did not like his friends, and his friends' friends were
impossible. Oxley's calls, on the other hand, were a
social triumph. He was punctiliously exclusive. Nobody else could even see him. When he came into
the room others often noticed that the room grew
suddenly and surprisingly chilly, but the author fails
to point out whether that was due to Lord Oxley's
station in life or after life.

Bit by bit the acquaintance between Frances and
the ghost ripened. At first she never looked at him
directly, but regarded his shadow in the mirror. And
they communicated only through music. Later
Frances made so bold as to speak to his lordship.

"When you first came," she said, her voice veiled,

husky, even a little broken, "I was afraid. I thought only of myself. I was terrified both at you and what you might demand from me. I hastened to leave this house, to go away and try to forget. But I wasn't permitted to forget. While I was away much concerning you was told me which changed my feeling toward you and showed me my duty. I have come back of my own free will. I am still afraid, but I no longer mind being afraid. My desire now is not to avoid, but rather to meet you. For, as I have learned, we are kinsfolk, you and I; and since this house is mine, you are in a sense my guest. Of that I have come to be glad. I claim you as part of my inheritance—the most valued, the most welcome portion, if you so will it. If I can help, serve, comfort you, I am ready to do so to the utmost of my poor capacity."

Alexis, Lord Oxley, made no reply, but it was evident that he accepted her offer of service and comfort graciously, for he continued to call regularly. His manners were perfect, although it is true that he never sent up his card, and yet in one matter Frances felt compelled to chide him and even tearfully implore a reformation. It made her nervous when she noticed one day that he carried in his right hand the ghost of the pistol with which he had shot himself. Agreeably he abandoned his century old habit, but later he was able to give more convincing proof of his regard for Frances. She was alone in the Tall Villa when her husband's vulgar friend, Morris Montagu, called. He came to tell her that her husband was behaving disgracefully in South Amer-

ica, and on the strength of that fact he made aggressive love. "Montagu's voice grew rasping and hoarse.
But before, paralyzed by disgust and amazement,
Frances had time to apprehend his meaning or combat his purpose, his coarse, pawlike—though much
manicured—hand grasped her wrist."

Suddenly the room grew chilly and Morris Montagu, in mortal terror, relaxed his grip and began to
run for the door as he cried, "Keep off, you ac-
cursed devil, I tell you. Don't touch me. Ah! Ah!
Damn you, keep off——"

It is evident to the reader that the ghost of Alexis,
Lord Oxley, is giving the vulgar fellow what used
to be known as "the bum's rush" in the days before
the Volstead act. At any rate, the voice of Montagu
grew feeble and distant and died away in the hall.
Then the front door slammed. Frances was saved!

After that, of course, it was evident to Alexis, Lord
Oxley, and Frances that they loved each other. He
began to talk to her in a husky and highfalutin style.
He even stood close to her chair and patted her head.
"Presently," writes Lucas Malet, "his hand dwelt
shyly, lingering upon her bent head, her cheek, the
nape of her slender neck. And Frances felt his hand
as a chill yet tender draw, encircling, playing upon
her. This affected her profoundly, as attacking her
in some sort through the medium of her senses, from
the human side, and thereby augmenting rather than
allaying the fever of her grief."

Naturally, things could not go on in that way forever, and so Alexis, Lord Oxley, arranged that
Frances should cross the bridge with him into the

next life. It was not difficult to arrange this. She had only to die. And so she did. All of which goes to prove that though it is well to be polite and well spoken to ghosts, they will bear watching as much as other men.

XL

PROFESSOR GEORGE PIERCE BAKER

A great many persons speak and write about Professor George Pierce Baker, of Harvard, as if he were a sort of agitator who made a practice of luring young men away from productive labor to write bad plays. There is no denying the fact that a certain number of dramatists have come out of Harvard's English 47, but the course also has a splendid record of cures. Few things in the world are so easy as to decide to write a play. It carries a sense of satisfaction entirely disproportionate to the amount of effort entailed. Even the failure to put a single line on paper brings no remorse, for it is easy to convince yourself that the thing would have had no chance in the commercial theater.

All this would be well enough except that the author of a phantom play is apt to remain a martyr throughout his life. He makes a very bad husband and father and a worse bridge partner. Freudians know the complaint as the Euripidean complex. The sufferer is ailing because his play lies suppressd in his subconscious mind.

Professor Baker digs these plays out. People who come to English 47 may talk about their plays as much as they choose, but they must write them, too.

Often a cure follows within forty-eight hours after the completion of a play. Sometimes it is enough for the author to read the thing through for himself, but if that does not avail there is an excellent chance for him after his play has been read aloud by Professor Baker and criticized by the class. If a pupil still wishes to write plays after this there is no question that he belongs in the business. He may, of course, never earn a penny at it but, starve or flourish, he is a playwright.

Professor Baker deserves the thanks of the community, then, not only for Edward Sheldon, and Cleves Kincaid, and Miss Lincoln and Eugene O'Neill and some of the other playwrights who came from English 47, but also for the number of excellent young men who have gone straight from his classroom to Wall Street, and the ministry, and automobile accessories with all the nascent enthusiasm of men just liberated from a great delusion.

In another respect Professor Baker has often been subjected to much undeserved criticism. Somebody has figured out that there are 2.983 more rapes in the average English 47 play than in the usual noncollegiate specimen of commercial drama. We feel comparatively certain that there is nothing in the personality of Professor Baker to account for this or in the traditions of Harvard, either. We must admit that nowhere in the world is a woman quite so unsafe as in an English 47 play, but the faculty gives no official encouragement to this undergraduate enthusiasm for sex problems. One must look beyond the Dean and the faculty for an explanation. It has something

to do with Spring, and the birds, and the saplings
and "What Every Young Man Ought to Know" and
all that sort of thing.

When I was in English 47 I remember that all
our plays dealt with Life. At that none of us regarded it very highly. Few respected it and certainly
no one was in favor of it. The course was limited
to juniors, seniors and graduate students and we were
all a little jaded. There were times, naturally, when
we regretted our lost illusions and longed to be fresh-
men again and to believe everything the Sunday newspapers said about Lillian Russell. But usually there
was no time for regrets; we were too busy telling Life
what we thought about it. Here there was a diver-
gence of opinion. Some of the playwrights in English 47 said that Life was a terrific tragedy. In
their plays the hero shot himself, or the heroine, or
both, as the circumstances might warrant, in the last
act. The opposing school held that Life was a joke,
a grim jest to be sure, cosmic rather than comic, but
still mirthful. The plays by these authors ended with
somebody ordering "Another small bottle of Pom-
mery" and laughing mockingly, like a world-wise
cynic.

Bolshevism had not been invented at that time,
but Capital was severely handled just the same. All
our villains were recruited from the upper classes.
Yet capitalism had an easy time of it compared with
marriage. I do not remember that a single play which
I heard all year in 47, whether from Harvard or
Radcliffe, had a single word of toleration, let alone
praise, for marriage. And yet it was dramatically

204

essential, for without marriage none of us would have been able to hammer out our dramatic tunes upon the triangle. Most of the epigrams also were about marriage. "Virtue is a polite word for fear," that is the sort of thing we were writing when we were not empowering some character to say, "Honesty is a bedtime fairy story invented for the proletariat," or "The prodigal gets drunk; the Puritan gets religion."

But up to date Professor Baker has stood up splendidly under this yearly barrage of epigrams. With his pupils toppling institutions all around him he has held his ground firmly and insisted on the enduring quality of the fundamental technic of the drama. When a pupil brings in a play in favor of polygamy, Baker declines to argue but talks instead about peripety. In other words, Professor Baker is wise enough to realize that it is impossible that he should furnish, or even attempt to mold in any way, the philosophy which his students bring into English 47 each year. If it is often a crude philosophy that is no fault of his. He can't attempt to tell the fledgling playwrights what things to say and, of course, he doesn't. English 47 is designed almost entirely to give a certain conception of dramatic form. Professor Baker "tries in the light of historical practice to distinguish the permanent from the impermanent in technic." He endeavors, "by showing the inexperienced dramatist how experienced dramatists have solved problems similar to his own, to shorten a little the time of apprenticeship."

When a man has done with Baker he has begun

to grasp some of the things he must not do in writing a play. With that much ground cleared all that he has to do is to acquire a knowledge of life, devise a plot and find a manager.

XLI

Next to putting a gold crown upon a man's head and announcing, "I create you emperor," no evil genius could serve him a worse turn than by giving him a blue pencil and saying: "Now you're a censor." Unfortunately mankind loves to possess the power of sitting in judgment. In some respects the life of a censor is more exhilarating than that of an emperor. The best the emperor can do is to snip off the heads of men and women, who are mere mortals. The censor can decapitate ideas which but for him might have lived forever. Think, for instance, of the extraordinary thrill which might come to a matter-of-fact individual living to-day in the city of Philadelphia if he happened to be the censor to whom the moving-picture version of "Macbeth" was submitted. His eye would light upon the subtitle "Give me the dagger," and, turning to the volume called "Rules and Standards," he would find among the prohibitions: "Pictures which deal at length with gun play, and the use of knives."

"That," one hears the censor crying in triumph, "comes out."

"But," we may fancy the producer objecting, "you

207

can't take that out; Shakespeare wrote it, and it belongs in the play."

"I don't care who wrote it," the censor could answer. "It can't be shown in Pennsylvania."

And it couldn't. The little fat man with the blue pencil—and censors always become fat in time—can stand with both his feet upon the face of posterity; he can look Fame in the eye and order her to quit trumpeting; he can line his wastebasket with the greatest notions which have stirred the mind of man. Like Joshua of old, he can command the sun and the moon to stand still until they have passed inspection. Cleanliness, it has been said, is next to godliness, but just behind comes the censor.

Perhaps you may object that the censor would do none of the things mentioned. Perhaps he wouldn't, but the Pennsylvania State Board of Censors of Motion Pictures has been sufficiently alive to the possibilities of what it might want to do in reëditing the classics to give itself, specifically, supreme authority over the judgment and the work of dead masters. Under Section 22 of "Standards of the Board" we find:

"That the theme or story of a picture is adapted from a publication, whether classical or not; or that portions of a picture follow paintings or other illustrations, is not a sufficient reason for the approval of a picture or portions of a picture."

As a matter of fact, it is pretty hard to see just how "Macbeth" could possibly come to the screen in Pennsylvania. It might be banned on any one of several counts. For instance, "Prolonged fighting

208

scenes will be shortened, and brutal fights will be wholly disapproved." Nobody can question that the murder of Banquo was brutal. "The use of profane and objectionable language in subtitles will be disapproved," which would handicap Macduff a good deal in laying on in his usual fashion.

"Gruesome and unduly distressing scenes will be disapproved. These include shooting, stabbing, profuse bleeding——" If Shakespeare had only written with Pennsylvania in mind, Duncan might be still alive and Lady Macbeth sleep as well as the next one.

But at this point we recognize another gentleman who wishes to protest against any more attacks upon motion-picture censorship being made which rest wholly on supposition. He has read "Standards of the Board," issued by the gentlemen in Pennsylvania, and he asserts that all the rules laid down are legitimate if interpreted with intelligence.

It will not be necessary to put the whole list of rules in evidence since there need be no dispute as to the propriety of such rules as prohibit moving pictures about white slavery and the drug traffic. Skipping these, we come to No. 5, which is as follows:

"Scenes showing the modus operandi of criminals which are suggestive and incite to evil action, such as murder, poisoning, housebreaking, safe robbery, pocket picking, the lighting and throwing of bombs, the use of ether, chloroform, etc., to render men and women unconscious, binding and gagging, will be disapproved."

Here I take the liberty of interrupting for a

moment to protest that the board has framed this rule upon the seeming assumption that to see murders, robberies, and the rest is to wish at once to emulate the criminals. This theory is in need of proving. "A good detective story" is the traditional relaxation of all men high in power in times of stress, but it is not recorded of Roosevelt, Wilson, Secretary of State Hughes, Lloyd George, nor of any of the other noted devotees of criminal literature that he attempted to put into practice any of the things of which he read. But to get on with the story:

"(6) Gruesome and unduly distressing scenes will be disapproved. These include shooting, stabbing, profuse bleeding, prolonged views of men dying and of corpses, lashing and whipping and other torture scenes, hangings, lynchings, electrocutions, surgical operations, and views of persons in delirium or insane."

Here, of course, a great deal is left to the discretion of the censors. Just what is "gruesome and unduly distressing"? This, I fancy, must depend upon the state of the censor's digestion. To a vegetarian censor it might be nothing more than a close-up of a beefsteak dinner. To a man living in the city which supports the Athletics and the Phillies a mere flash of a baseball game might be construed as "gruesome and unduly distressing."

This is another of the rules which puts Shakespeare in his place, sweeping out, as it does, both Lear and Ophelia. And possibly Hamlet. Was Hamlet mad? The Pennsylvania censors will have to take that question up in a serious way sooner or later.

"(7) Studio and other scenes, in which the human form is shown in the nude, or the body is unduly exposed, will be disapproved."

This fails to state whether the prohibition includes the reproduction of statues shown publicly and familiarly to all comers in our museums.

Prohibition No. 8, which deals with eugenics, birth control and similar subjects, may be passed without comment, as it refers rather to news than to feature pictures.

Prohibition No. 9 covers a wide field:

"Stories or scenes holding up to ridicule and reproach races, classes, or other social groups, as well as the irreverent and sacrilegious treatment of religious bodies or other things held to be sacred, will be disapproved."

Here we have still another rule which might be invoked against Hamlet's coming to the screen, since the chance remark, "Something is rotten in the state of Denmark," might logically be held to be offensive to Scandinavians. "The Merchant of Venice," of course, would have no chance, not only as anti-Semitic propaganda, but because it holds up money lenders, a well-known social group, to ridicule.

No. 10 briefly forbids pictures which deal with counterfeiting, seemingly under the impression that if this particular crime is never mentioned the members of the underworld may possibly forget its existence. In No. 11 there is the direct prohibition of "scenes showing men and women living together without marriage." Here the greatest difficulty will fall upon those film manufacturers who deal in travel pictures. No exhibitor is safe in flashing upon a screen the picture of a cannibal man and woman and several little cannibals in front of their hut without first ascertaining from the camera man that he went inside and inspected the wedding certificate. No. 13 forbids the use of "profane and objectionable language," which we shall find later has been construed to include the simple "Hell."

Under 15 we find this ruling: "Views of incendiarism, burning, wrecking, and the destruction of property, which may put like action into the minds of those of evil instincts, or may degrade the morals of the young, will be disapproved."

In other words, Nero may fiddle to his heart's content, but he must do it without the inspiration of the burning of Rome. Curiously enough, throughout all the rules of censorship there runs a continuous train of reasoning that the pictures must be adapted to the capacity and mentality of the lowest possible person who could wander into a picture house. The picture-loving public, in the minds of the censors, seems to be honeycombed with potential murderers, incendiaries, and counterfeiters. Rule No. 16 discourages scenes of drunkenness, and adds chivalrously: "Especially if women have a part in the scenes."

Next we come to a rule which would handicap vastly any attempt to reproduce Stevenson or any other lover of the picaresque upon the screen. "Pictures which deal at length with gun play," says Rule 17, "and the use of knives, and are set in the underworld, will be disapproved. Prolonged fighting scenes will be shortened and brutal fights will be wholly disapproved."

What, we wonder, would the censors do with a picture about Thermopylæ? Would they, we wonder, command that resistance be shortened if the picture was to escape the ban? The Alamo was another fight which dragged on unduly, and Grant was guilty of great disrespect in his famous "If it takes all summer," not to mention the impudent incitement toward the prolongation of a fight in Lawrence's "Don't give up the ship."

No. 19 suggests difficulties in its ban on "sensual kissing and love-making scenes." Naturally the question arises: "At just what point does a kiss become sensual?" Here the censors, to their credit, have been clear and definite in their ruling. They have decided that a kiss remains chaste for ten feet. If held upon the screen for as much as an inch above this limit, it changes character and becomes sensual. Here, at any rate, morality has been measured with an exactitude which is rare.

No. 20 is puzzling. It begins, liberally enough, with the announcement that "Views of women smoking will not be disapproved as such," but then adds belatedly that this ruling does not apply if "their manner of smoking is suggestive." Suggestive of what, I wonder? Perhaps the censors mean that it is all right for women to smoke in moving pictures if only they don't inhale, but it would have been much more simple to have said just that. No. 22 is the famous proclamation that the classics, as well as other themes, must meet Pennsylvania requirements, and in 23 we have a fine general rule which covers almost anything a censor may want to do. "Themes or incidents in picture stories," it reads, "which are designed to inflame the mind to improper adventures, or to establish false standards of conduct, coming under the foregoing classes, or of other kinds, will be disapproved. Pictures will be judged as a whole, with a view to their final total effect; those portraying evil in any form which may be easily remembered or emulated will be disapproved."

Perhaps there are still some who remain unconvinced as to the excesses of censorship. The argument may be advanced that nothing is wrong with the rules mentioned if only they are enforced with discretion and intelligence. In answer to this plea the best thing to do would be to consider a few of the eliminations in definite pictures which were required by the Pennsylvania board and by the one in Ohio which operates under a somewhat similar set of regulations. An industrial play called "The Whistle" was banned in its entirety in Pennsylvania under the following ruling: "Disapproved under Section 6 of the Act of 1915. Symbolism of the title raises class antagonism and hatred, and throughout subtitles, scenes, and incidents have the same effect."

But most astounding of all was the final observation: "Child-labor and factory laws of this State would make incident shown impossible." In other words, if a thing did not happen in Pennsylvania it is assumed not to have happened at all. It is entirely possible that the next producer who brings an Indian picture to the censors may be asked to eliminate the elephants on the ground that "there aren't any in this State."

The same State ordered out of "Officer Cupid," a comedy, a scene in which one of the chief comedians was seen robbing a safe, presumably under the section against showing crime upon the stage.

Most troublesome of all were the changes ordered into the screen version of Augustus Thomas's well-known play "The Witching Hour." It may be remembered that the villain of this piece was an assistant district attorney in the State of Kentucky, but Pennsylvania would not have him so. It is difficult to find any specific justification for this attitude in the published standards of the State unless we assume that a district attorney was classified as belonging to the group "other things held to be sacred" which were not to be treated lightly. The first ruling of the censors in regard to "The Witching Hour" ran: "Reel One—Eliminate subtitle 'Frank Hardmuth, assistant district attorney,' and substitute 'Frank Hardmuth, a prosperous attorney.' "

Next came: "Reel Two—Eliminate subtitle, 'I can give her the best—money, position, and, as far as character—I am district attorney now, and before you know it I will be the governor,' and substitute: 'I can give her the best—money, position, and, as far as character—I am now a prosperous attorney, and before you know it I will be running for governor.' "

And again: "Eliminate subtitle: 'Exactly—but you have taken an oath to stand by this city,' and substitute: 'Exactly, but you have taken an oath to stand by the law.' "

PIECES OF HATE

This curious complex that even assistant district attorneys should be above suspicion ran through the entire film. Simpler was the change of the famous curtain line which was familiar to all theatergoers of New York ten or twelve seasons ago when "The Witching Hour" was one of the hits of the season. It may be remembered that at the end of the third act Frank Hardmuth, then a district attorney and not yet reduced to a prosperous attorney, ran into the library of the hero to kill him. The hero's name we have forgotten, but he was a professional gambler, of a high type, who later turned hypnotist. Hardmuth thrust a pistol into his stomach, and we can still see the picture and hear the line as John Mason turned and said: "You can't shoot that gun [and then after a long pause]: You can't even hold it." Hardmuth, played by George Nash, staggered back and exclaimed, just before the curtain came down: "I'd like to know how in Hell you did that to me." It can hardly have been equally effective in moving pictures after the censor made the caption read: "I'd like to know how you did that to me." The original version fell under the ban against profanity.

In Ohio a more recent picture called "The Gilded Lily" had not a little trouble. Here the Board of Censors curtly ordered: "First Reel—Cut out girl smoking cigarette which she takes from man." Seemingly they did not even stop to consider whether or not she smoked it suggestively. And again in the third reel came the order: "Cut out all scenes of girl's smoking cigarette at table." Most curious of all was the order: "Cut out verse with words: 'I'm

216

a little prairie flower growing wilder every hour.' "

William Vaughn Moody's "The Faith Healer" was considered a singularly dignified and moving play in its dramatic form, but the picture ran into difficulties, as usual, in Pennsylvania. "Eliminate subtitle," came the order: " 'Your power is not gone because you love—but because your love has fallen on one unworthy.' " As this is a fair statement of the idea upon which Mr. Moody built his play, it cannot be said that anything which the moving-picture producers brought in was responsible.

Throughout the rest of the world one may thumb his nose as a gesture of scorn and contempt, but in Pennsylvania this becomes a public menace not to be tolerated. "Reel Two"—we find in the records of the Board of Censors—"eliminate view of man thumbing his nose at lion."

As a matter of fact, no rule of censorship of any sort may be framed so wisely that by and by some circumstance will not arise under which it may be turned to an absurd use. Any censors must have rules. No man can continue to make decisions all day long. He must eventually fall back upon the bulwark of printed instructions. I observed an instance of this sort during the war. A rule was passed forbidding the mention of any arrivals from America in France. An American captain who had brought his wife to France ran into this regulation when he attempted to cable home to his parents the news that he had become the proud parent of a son. "Charles Jr. arrived to-day. Weight eight pounds. Everything fine," he wrote on the cable blank, only to have it turned back to him with the information: "We're not allowed to pass any messages about arrivals."

It is almost as difficult for babies to arrive in motion-picture stories. Any suggestion which would tend to weaken the faith of any one in storks or cabbage leaves is generally frowned upon. For a time picture producers felt that they had discovered a safe device which would inform adults and create no impression in the minds of younger patrons, and pictures were filled with mothers knitting baby clothes. This has now been ruled out as quite too shocking. "Eliminate scene showing Bobby holding up baby's sock," the Pennsylvania body has ruled, "and scene showing Bobby standing with wife kissing baby's sock." In fact, there is nothing at all to be done except to make all screen babies so many Topsies who never were born at all. Even such a simple sentence as "And Julia Duane faced the most sacred duties of a woman's life alone" was barred.

Like poor Julia Duane, the moving-picture producers have one problem which they must face alone. They are confronted with difficulties unknown to the publisher of books and the producer of plays. The movie man must frame a story which will interest grown-ups and at the same time contain nothing which will disturb the innocence of the youngest child in the audience. At any rate, that is the task to which he is held by most censorship boards. The publisher of a novel knows that there are certain things which he may not permit to reach print without being liable to prosecution, but at the same time he knows that he is perfectly safe in allowing many things in his book

218

which are not suitable for a four-year-old-child. There is no prospect that the four-year-old child will read it. Just so when a manager undertakes a production of Ibsen's "Ghosts" it never enters into his head just what its effect will be on little boys of three. But these same youngsters will be at the picture house, and the standards of what is suitable for them must be standards of all the others. There should, of course, be some way of grading movie houses. There should be theaters for children under fourteen, others with subjects suitable for spectators from fourteen to sixty, and then small select theaters for those more than sixty in which caution might be thrown to the winds.

Another of the difficulties of the unfortunate moving-picture producer is the fact that censorship bodies in various parts of the country have a faculty of seldom hitting on the same thing as objectionable. There is, of course, a National Association of the Motion Picture Industry which maintains its own censorship through which 92 per cent of all the pictures exhibited in America are passed, but in addition to that Pennsylvania, Ohio, Kansas, and Maryland have State censorship boards, and there are numerous local bodies as well. Cecil B. De Mille complained, shortly after his version of Geraldine Farrar in "Carmen" was launched, that at that time there were approximately thirty-five censorship organizations in the United States. These included various State and municipal boards. Every one of these thirty-odd organizations censored "Carmen." No two boards censored the same thing. In other words, what was

219

morally accept ble to New York was highly immoral in Pennsylvani . What Pennsylvania might see with impunity was onsidered dangerous to the citizens of an adjoining ate.

Of course question at issue is whether the potential immora picture shall first be shown at the producer's or t e exhibitor's risk, or whether censorship shall com first before there has been any public showing. The contention is made by some of the moving-picture people that they should have the same freedom given o people who deal in print to publish first and take he consequences later if any statute has been violat d. The right to free speech, in fact, has been invo ed in favor of the motion picture as a medium of xpression. This view had the support of the late Mayor Gaynor, an excellent jurist, but apparently it i not the view held by various State courts which h ve passed upon the constitutionality of censorship l ws. When the aldermen of New York City passed a ordinance providing for the censorship of movies Mayor Gaynor wrote: "If this ordinance is legal, hen a similar ordinance in respect of the newspaper and the theaters generally would be legal. Once r vive the censorship and there is no telling how fa we may carry it."

No matter w at the law, the real basis of censorship is the public i self. Persons who feel that tighter lines of censo hip must be drawn and new bodies established go on the theory that there is a great demand for th salacious moving-picture show. But there is no co inuing appeal in dirt in the theater. It does not pe anently sell the biggest of the maga-

220

zines or the newspapers. And naturally it is not a paying commodity to the moving-picture men. The best that the censor can do is to guess what will be offensive to the general public. The general public can be much more accurate in its reactions. It knows. And it is prepared to stay away from the dirty show in droves.

CENSORING THE CENSOR

Mice and anaries were sometimes employed in France to de ect the presence of gas. When these little things egan to die in their cages the soldiers knew that th air had become dangerous. Some such system s ould be devised for censorship to make it practical. Even with the weight of authority behind him no bland person, with virtue obviously unruffled, is a together convincing when he announces that the book he has just read or the moving picture he has seen s so hideously immoral that it constitutes a dang r to the community. For my part I always feel t at if he can stand it so can I. To the best of my k owledge and belief, Mr. Sumner was not swayed fr m his usual course of life by so much as a single pe cadillo for all of *Jurgen*. His indignation was alto ther altruistic. He feared for the fate of weaker m and women.

Every the rical manager, every motion picture producer, an every publisher knows, to his sorrow, that the busin ss of estimating the effect of any piece of imaginativ work upon others is precarious and uncertain. nius would be required to predict accurately the eaction of the general public to any set piece whi h seems immoral to the censor. For instance, why was Mr. Sumner so certain that *Jurgen*, which inspired him with horror and loathing, would prove a persuasive temptation to all the rest of the world? Censorship is serious and drastic business; it should never rest merely upon guesswork and more particularly not upon the guesses of men so staunch in morals that they are obviously of distant kin to the rest of humanity.

The censor should be a person of a type capable of being blasted for the sins of the people. His job can be elevated to dignity only when the world realizes that he runs horrid risks. If we should choose our censors from fallible folk we might have proof instead of opinions. Suppose the censor of *Jurgen* had been some one other than Mr. Sumner, some one so unlike the head of the vice society that after reading Mr. Cabell's book he had come out of his room, not quivering with rage, but leering and wearing vine leaves. In such case the rest would be easy. It would merely be necessary to shadow the censor until he met his first dryad. His wink would be sufficient evidence and might serve as a cue for the rescuers to rush forward and save him. Of course there would then be no necessity for legal proceedings in regard to the book. Expert testimony as to its possible effects would be irrelevant. We would know and we could all join cheerfully in the bonfire.

To my mind there are three possible positions which may logically be taken concerning censorship. It might be entrusted to the wisest man in the world, to a series of average men,—or be abolished. Unfortunately it as been our experience that there is a distinct affini between fools and censorship. It seems to be ne of those treading grounds where they rush in. To be sure, we ought to admit a prejudice at the o tset and acknowledge that we were a reporter in F ance during the war at a time when censors seeme a little more ridiculous than usual. We still rem mber the young American lieutenant who held up story of a boxing match in Saint-Nazaire because e reporter wrote, "In the fourth round MacBeth land d a nice right on the Irishman's nose and the claret began to flow." "I'm sorry," said the censor, "but w have strict orders from Major Palmer that no mentio of wine or liquor is to be allowed in any story abo t the American army."

Nor have e forgotten the story of General Petain's must che. "Why," asked Junius Wood of the *Globe,* "h ve you held up my story? All the rest have gon ."

"Unfortuna ely," answered the courteous Frenchman, "you ha e twice used the expression General Petain's 'whit mustache.' I might stretch a point and let you s 'gray mustache,' but I should much prefer to have you say 'blond mustache.'"

"Oh, make i green with purple spots," said Junius.

The use of verage men in censorship would necessitate sacrifice to the persuasive seduction of immorality, as I have suggested, and moreover there are very few average men. Accordingly, I am prepared to a andon that plan of censorship. The wisest man in he world is too old and two busy with his plays and as announced that he will never come

224

to America. Accordingly we venture to suggest that in time of peace we try to get along without any censorship of plays or books or moving pictures. I have no desire, of course, to leave Mr. Sumner unemployed—it would ·perhaps be only fair to allow him to slosh around among the picture post cards.

Once official censorship had been officially abolished, a strong and able censorship would immediately arise consisting of the playgoing and read-. ing public. It is a rather offensive error to assume that the vast majority of folk in America are rarin' to get to dirty books and dirty plays. It is the experience of New York managers that the run of the merely salacious play is generally short. The success which a few nasty books have had has been largely because of the fact that they came close to the line of things which are forbidden. Without the prohibition there would be little popularity.

To save myself from the charge of hypocrisy I should add that personally I believe there ought to be a certain amount of what we now know as immoral writing. It would do no harm in a community brought up to take it or let it alone. It is well enough for the reading public and the critic to use terms such as moral or immoral, but they hardly belong in the vocabulary of an artist. I have heard it said that before Lucifer left Heaven there were no such things as virtues and vices. The world was equipped with a certain number of traits which were qualities without distinction or shame. But when Lucifer and the heavenly hosts drifted into their eternal warfare it was agreed that each side should recruit an

225

equal number of these human, and at that time un-classified, qu ities. A coin was tossed and, whether by fair chanc or sharp miracle, Heaven won.

"I choose lessedness," said the Captain of the Angels. It s ould be explained that the selection was made wit out previous medical examination, and Blessedness s med at that time a much more robust recruit than e has since turned out to be. A ten-dency to flat f ot is always hard to detect.

"Give me eauty," said Lucifer, and from that day to this th artists of the world have been divided into two camp —those who wished to achieve beauty and those wh wished to achieve blessedness, those who wanted t make the world better and those who were indiffer t to its salvation if they could only succeed in ma ing it a little more personable.

However, e conflict is not quite so simple as that. Late in the afternoon when the Captain of the Angels had icked Unselfishness and Moderation and Faith an Hope and Abstinence, and Lucifer had called to is side Pride and Gluttony and Anger and Lust and Tactlessness, there remained only two more qualitie to be apportioned to the contending sides. One o them was Sloth, who was obviously overweight, a d the other was a furtive little fellow with his cap d wn over his eyes.

"What's y ur name?" said the Captain of the Angels.

"Truth," st mmered the little fellow.

"Speak up, ' said the Captain of the Angels so sharply that cifer remonstrated, saying, "Hold on there; Anger's on my side."

"Truth," said the little fellow again but with the same somewhat indistinct utterance which has always been so puzzling to the world.

"I don't understand you," said the Captain of the Angels, "but if it's between you and Sloth I'll take a chance with you. Stop at the locker room and get your harp and halo."

Now to-day even Lucifer will admit, if you get him in a corner, that Truth is the mightiest warrior of them all. The only trouble is his truancy. Sometimes he can't be found for centuries. Then he will bob up unexpectedly, break a few heads, and skip away. Nothing can stand against him. Lucifer's best ally, Beauty, is no match for him. Truth holds every decision. But the trouble is that he still keeps his cap down over his eyes, and he still mumbles his words, and nobody knows him until he is at least fifty years away and moving fast. At that distance he seems to grow bigger, and he invariably reaches into his back pocket and puts on his halo so that people can recognize him. Still, when he comes along the next time and is face to face with any man of this world, the mortal is pretty sure to say, "Your face is familiar but I can't seem to place you."

There is no denying that he isn't a good mixer. But for that he would be an excellent censor.